HEALING

HOW TO BE HEALED AND HOW TO HEAL THE SICK

Exodus 15 v 26
"I am the Lord who heals you"

Pastor Anne Simpson-Phillipson

Sunesis Ministries Ltd

Healing: How to Be Healed and How to Heal the Sick

Copyright © 2014 Anne Simpson-Phillipson.

The right of Anne Simpson-Phillipson to be identified as the author of this work has been asserted by her in accordance with the Copyright, Designs, and Patents Act 1988.

The author guarantees all contents are original and do not infringe upon the legal rights of any other person or work. All rights reserved. No part of this publication may be reproduced or transmitted in any form or by any means, electronic or mechanical, including photocopy, recording, or any information storage and retrieval system, without permission in writing from the author.

The author of this book does not dispense medical advice or prescribe the use of any technique as a form of treatment for physical, emotional, or medical problems without the advice of a physician, either directly or indirectly. The intent of the author is only to offer information of a general nature to help you in your quest for emotional and spiritual well-being. In the event you use any of the information in this book for yourself, the author and publisher assume no responsibility for your actions. The views expressed in this book are solely those of the author and do not necessarily reflect the views of the publisher, and the publisher hereby disclaims any responsibility for them.

ISBN: 978-0-9928495-2-8

Unless otherwise indicated, Biblical quotations are from the HOLY BIBLE, NEW INTERNATIONAL VERSION. Copyright © 1973, 1978, 1984 by International Bible Society. Used by permission of Hodder and Stoughton Ltd, a member of the Hodder Headline Plc Group. All rights reserved. "NIV" is a registered trademark of International Bible Society. UK trademark number 1448790.

Quotations marked KJV are from the Holy Bible, King James Version.

Published by Sunesis Ministries Ltd
Email: info@stuartpattico.com
Website: www.stuartpattico.com

CONTENTS

INTRODUCTION   5

SECTION 1 - HOW TO BE HEALED

CHAPTER 1 - THE ORIGIN OF SICKNESS   9
Where did sickness come from? What are the sources of sickness?

CHAPTER 2 - THE WORK OF THE CROSS   19
The price is paid.

CHAPTER 3 - THE MINISTRY OF JESUS   27
How did Jesus confront sickness?

CHAPTER 4 - MISUNDERSTANDING ABOUT HEALING   51
Is it always God's will to heal, what about Paul's Thorn? And many more questions explained

CHAPTER 5 - DIFFERENT TYPES OF HEALING   59
Creative miracles, emotional healing and deliverance
Barriers to healing
Holding on to your healing

SECTION 2 - HOW TO HEAL THE SICK

CHAPTER 6 - HOW DID JESUS AND THE APOSTLES HEAL THE SICK?   85
Do we carry the same authority?

CHAPTER 7 - THE HOLY SPIRIT AND HEALING   105

INTRODUCTION

Exodus 15 v 26 "I am the Lord who heals you"

Right from the beginning of creation, God has always been a healing God. His intention was always that his children should be healed and live in health. Throughout this book we will look at various aspects of healing including; what is the origin of sickness? Why do people get sick? What can we do practically to stay healthy? Has healing been purchased on the cross? Is it always the will of God to heal people? What are the barriers to healing? Can God use me to heal the sick? And much more.

We will look at the way that Jesus treated sickness and how he came with compassion for those who were suffering but not just with compassion, he came with an answer of healing, restoration and deliverance.

Hebrews 13 v 8 "Jesus Christ is the same, yesterday today and forever"

The same Jesus who walked on the earth and healed all who came to him is the same Jesus who is still healing the sick through the finished work of the cross. It is his will for us to be healed and for his people to also take his healing power to the world. God has not changed, his word has not changed and his promises are the same today.

Malachi 3 v 6 "I the Lord do not change"

We will also look at some misunderstandings concerning healing such as; what was Paul's thorn in the flesh? Is this sickness for God's glory? God will heal me in his time? Miracles are not for today? Many people have been discouraged from seeking and believing for healing because of a wrong teaching concerning healing and we will seek to look at what the bible has to say concerning these things.

I believe that we are living in a time where faith is rising to a new level and where the anointing is being poured out in a new way and in my own personal life and ministry, I have been seeing more people healed now than ever before. I want to say at the start of this book that I do not have all the answers as to why some people are not healed. I know some people who had great faith and yet they still died. I do not know the answers to these things but all I do know is this; Jesus told us to go and heal the sick and if we allow the things that we don't understand to hold us back then no-body will be healed but if we go in the understanding and faith that we have then I believe that more and more people will be healed. The ones that we don't understand we have to ask God for grace in what we do not understand and to allow him to heal the hurts and disappointments in our lives and to bring fresh hope and revelation for the future.

SECTION 1 - HOW TO BE HEALED

CHAPTER 1

ORIGINS OF SICKNESS

Why do people get sick? What is the source of sickness?

Genesis 1 v 26 God said "let us make man in our image".

When God created man he created him in his own image, in his likeness and so we need to ask the question; is God ever sick? God can not be sick, he is immortal, he can never die; therefore God does not have the ability within him to be sick. If we are created in God's image, then we were created to be healthy, to not have sickness or pain in our lives.

Genesis 1 v 31 "God saw all that he had made and it was very good".

Sickness is not good, it is painful, it brings death, it brings limitations. Therefore sickness can never be classed as being good and it does not come from God's original plan for our lives. Man was never supposed to die, we were created to live forever. I believe that is why we find death so hard to cope with. We can not understand how we have loved someone all our lives and now they are no longer there. I believe that the reason why we find death so hard to cope with is not only because of our sadness at losing someone close to us; but it is also because deep inside our spirits we feel that it is wrong; we were not supposed to die.

In Genesis 3 we read about the fall of man when they were deceived by the serpent and ate from the tree of the knowledge of good and evil. At that point sin entered into the world and death and sickness came into mankind. In v 19 God declared to the man "for dust you are and to dust you will return".

There at that point death, sickness and decay came into existence for the first time. Man was told that because of his disobedience that he would return to the earth after his days were finished, that he would no longer be allowed to eat from the tree of life and live forever. Man was banished from the garden where the tree of life was. I believe that this was actually God's grace; because if he had been allowed to eat from the tree of life at that point then man would have remained forever in his sinful state.

Genesis 3 v 22 "He must not be allowed to reach out his hand and take also from the tree of life and eat and live forever".

Genesis 3 v 24 "after he drove the man out, he placed on the east side of the Garden of Eden cherubim and a flaming sword flashing back and forth to guard the way to the tree of life".

God declares that man shall not be allowed to reach out to the tree of life and so he posted cherubim to guard the way to the tree of life preventing man from eating from it.

Revelation 2 v 7 "to him who overcomes, he will give the right to eat from the tree of life that is in the paradise of God".

The tree of life is still in the paradise of God and one day those who follow Jesus will be able to eat of it again and receive eternal life. One day death will be completely destroyed and we shall live forever with no more pain or suffering. God will restore the Paradise of God that was lost. Although we are waiting for the full restoration to take place, I believe that there are some things that have already been provided for us here on earth.

When Jesus went to the cross, he became a curse for us (Galatians 3 v 13-14) so that we might enter into the blessings of God. Today because of the cross, we no longer need to stay under the curse of sickness, we have been redeemed and we can enter in to the blessing of healing. One day we will enter in to the paradise of God and we will have new glorified bodies that will never age or die again (1 Corinthians 15 v 42-53). In the meantime we live in bodies that will die one day but they will only die so that we can be clothed with our new resurrected bodies that will live forever with no more pain or death. God is restoring everything back that was lost in the fall. However, just because our natural bodies have to die one day, I do not believe that we have to be sick to die. We can just go peacefully when it is our time to go. Moses was 120 years old when he died and yet his eyes were not dim, nor his strength gone (Deuteronomy 34 v 7).

If that was possible under the Old Testament, then how much more under the new testament promises, can we live healthy lives right up to old age. In 2 Corinthians 3 v 7-11 it speaks of how the old testament covenant is dull in comparison to the glory of the New Covenant. When Jesus hung on the cross, he not only took all of our sins, but he also took all of our infirmities and by his wounds we are healed (Isaiah 53 4-5).

So we can see that the origin and the source of sickness was because of the fall of man but now because of the cross, that curse has been broken and today full healing and restoration is available to every believer and even though our bodies will have to die, they don't have to be sick to die. Just like Moses, we can be taken home in full health when we have finished all that we have to do here on earth. The only reason that we have to die is so that we can be clothed with our new glorified body.

Wrong Lifestyle

Another reason that we can be sick is because we have not taken correct responsibility for our lives.

1 Corinthians 6 v 19 "do you not know that your body is a temple of the Holy Spirit".

God has given us a plan for healing for our bodies but he has also given us the ability to make right or wrong choices as to how we look after our bodies on this earth. We can decide to do things that will help to keep us healthy or we can choose to do things that neglect our health. I began to think about this some time ago as I was going to different meetings and praying for people for healing. So as I began to ask the Lord about this; he directed me to do a teaching session on healthy living. Sometimes we can just focus on the spiritual aspects and forget about the natural; but God has called us to be spiritual beings but living in natural bodies at this time so we have to look after both of them. Nearly every day you can read in the newspaper that a third of all cancers could be prevented if we just led a more healthy life. Therefore prevention is better than cure. God would prefer us to live in health rather than to have to keep asking for healing and I believe that there are some practical things that we can do to help us to stay healthy

3 John v 2 "I pray that you may enjoy good health.

I can not say that I am always doing the right things and I do still like to eat foods that are probably not healthy sometimes. If we become too strict, then we can become fed up and end up binging out on things instead, so I believe that it is everything in moderation. We need to make sure that we keep to a sensible weight and to give our bodies good exercise on a regular basis - walking is always good and it costs nothing and you can do it almost anywhere with very little preparation involved apart from putting on your shoes! Getting a dog is always a good way to encourage you to go for a walk although this may not be practical for everyone. If you are not able to walk at the moment due to an illness, then find another more gentle exercise that you can do; even if it is very small movements from your chair, anything that raises your heart rate slightly is good for you. I believe that the key is to find something that you enjoy; because if you enjoy it, then you are more likely to keep it up.

Eating some good food and especially fruit and vegetables is also good for you. For the past few years I have tried to make up fruit smoothies in the morning and I can say that I have felt a lot better for it. Many fruits have anti-oxidants in them which help to fight against many illnesses and they boost your immune system helping your body to fight off any germs that are trying to attack your body. Our bodies are the temple of the Holy Spirit and while we are on earth, this is the only body that we are going to have to be able to live our lives in and to serve God with, so I believe that we have a responsibility to look after the body that we have been given at this time. If we have been called for a purpose here on earth, then we need to be healthy so that we can fulfil all that God wants us to do.

Wrong Emotions

As well as practical things for our body, there is also the emotional state of us as well which can greatly affect our body. If we live constantly up-tight and anxious and worrying all the time, then this will raise our blood pressure which can lead to all kinds of strokes and heart conditions. We need to bring all our cares to the Lord so that we can walk in the peace of the Lord which will bring healing to our physical bodies. Along with emotional things, we sometimes have bitterness, un-forgiveness, anger, resentment and I have known these things to be a root to arthritis and other nerve and joint problems in people's lives. If we live our lives feeling twisted up inside then it will also manifest itself in the twisting of our bodies as well.

Proverbs 14 v 30 "envy rots the bones".
Proverbs 17 v 22 " a cheerful heart is good medicine but a crushed spirit dries up the bones".

Proverbs 13 v 12 "hope deferred makes the heart sick".

We need to allow those wrong emotions to be taken by the Lord and to learn to release forgiveness so that we can release ourselves. When we choose to hold on to un-forgiveness and resentment then the only person that we really hurt is ourselves. But when we choose to release those things to God, then he will deal with them and we will be free to enjoy our lives free from pain. When you feel yourself getting angry and irritated, you can feel your whole body tensing up and if we live our whole lives with a tensed up body, then it will greatly affect our physical health.

Philippians 4 v 6 "Do not be anxious about anything but in everything by prayer and petition present your requests to God with thanksgiving. And the peace of God that transcends all understanding will guard your heart and mind in Christ Jesus".

God says that we should hand over all our anxieties and the things that would weigh us down and burden us. We should hand all these things to the Lord and as we do so, he will give us his peace that will guard our hearts and our minds. Similarly if we are harbouring bitter thoughts in our hearts, then these can also release the wrong kind of chemicals into our bodies allowing sickness to come into our bodies. We can not help the thoughts and the emotions that come to us at different times when we are going through difficult situations but when those things come, we can choose whether we continue to hold on to them or whether we choose to hand them over to the Lord asking him to instead give us his grace to let go and to walk in his peace. The peace of the Lord is one of the greatest gifts that we can have - there is nothing to compare with having the peace of God in your life. Jesus said "my peace I give to you, not as the world gives". The world can only give us temporal peace according to our circumstances, but Jesus' peace is based on his presence not on circumstances. We can have peace even in the midst of the storm, because Jesus is there with us and letting us know that he is in control of the storm. When we allow Jesus into our storms, he calms them, he calms our minds, our hearts, our emotions and keeps us in perfect peace.

Generational

Some people are ill because of a sickness that is running in a family line. Many people who suffer with heart conditions or cancers will tell you that their mother or grand mother also suffered with those things too. It is a medical fact that illnesses do run in family lines but because of the cross, we do not need to live under the curse of any generational sickness. We have a new blood line - it is the blood of Jesus so we can reject the wrong things that have come down our natural blood line and instead enter into the blessing of the blood of Jesus.

Deuteronomy 28 v 15-48 lists all of the curses for disobedience and as you read that list you will find listed there many different sicknesses both physical, emotional and mental but the good news is that Jesus became a curse for us so that we can inherit a blessing. We don't need to stay under a generational curse, we can claim the healing and restoration from the cross. We also need to be careful about the words that we speak over our lives because sometimes we can also curse ourselves with the words that we speak. Sometimes we hear people saying things like this; "Well, my mother had a heart attack when she was 50, so I expect that I will be getting one soon". Jesus said "according to your faith, be it unto you". You can choose to have faith for negative things or positive things. If you believe that you are going to have a heart attack, then you are believing and expecting and setting yourself up for the devil to bring that into your life. Then when it happens we say "Oh there we are, the generational line is continuing"! but it doesn't need to continue because when Jesus went to the cross he declared "it is finished". The old order of things has finished and we have entered into a new covenant because of the blood of Jesus. Jesus has purchased our healing, our deliverance, our restoration to live in health.

CHAPTER 2 - THE WORK OF THE CROSS

It is Finished

John 19 v 30. When Jesus hung on the cross, he cried out those famous words "it is finished". Those who were standing around may have misunderstood what he meant as he cried out those words. They may have assumed that he was saying "I am finished, I am dying", but that was not what he meant at all. When he cried out those words, it was the cry of the greatest victory ever known in the history of the world. The words are literally translated from a Hebrew word "Tetelestai" which was a word that was written on business documents or receipts in New Testament times to show that a bill had been paid in full. It comes from a Greek verb "teleo" which means; to bring to an end, to complete, to fulfil, to accomplish (so that the thing done corresponds to what has been said). Therefore when Jesus cried out "tetelestai"- It is finished - he was saying "I have paid the price in full, I have completed my mission, the debt has been paid, I have fulfilled all that I came to do". We need to understand that just as salvation and the forgiveness of sins was paid for at the cross, so also the price for our healing and wholeness was purchased at the cross. The two things go together and can not be separated. Jesus came to purchase salvation for the whole person - body, soul and spirit.

The word salvation actually comes from a Greek word "sozo" which means - to save, deliver, protect, heal, preserve, do well and be made whole. So when Jesus said that if we believe in him, we shall be saved; he was literally saying that we shall be saved, delivered, protected, preserved, healed and made whole! You can not separate healing from salvation because it comes in the whole package. When you buy a holiday package, you get the flight, the transfer and the accommodation all in one package and so at the cross you get the whole package if you will believe and receive it. Therefore when we get a revelation of the finished work of the cross, we will realise that healing has already been purchased and instead of asking God to heal us, we will instead be thanking him for the finished work and reaching out by faith to receive what he has already done. Let us look at the passage in Isaiah 53 concerning the prophecy of the cross and see what the prophet was prophesying concerning the work of the cross.

Isaiah 53 v 4 "Surely he took up our infirmities and carried our sorrows"

The KJV says "surely he has borne our griefs" and the Hebrew word for "griefs" is choliy; pronounced "kohl-ee" and it literally means - anxiety, calamity, disease, sickness, grief. So here in this one word we have healing for body, mind and emotions. Isaiah prophesied that when the Messiah came that he would take upon himself all of our anxieties, diseases, sicknesses and grief and sorrows.

V 5 "he was pierced for our transgressions and crushed for our iniquities"
(KJV) "he was wounded for our transgressions, he was bruised for our iniquities".

The word transgression comes from a Hebrew word "pesha" which means - a revolt, rebellion. All of us have rebelled against God and need his forgiveness - he took our rebellion upon himself so that we can be reconciled back to God (2 Corinthians 5 v 19) Christ was reconciling the world back to himself, not counting men's sins against them. After the fall man was banished from God's presence because of their rebellion and sin and was destined to live outside the blessing of God, but Jesus came to pay the price for our rebellion, he took our punishment and by his blood we are restored back into a right relationship with God.

The word iniquities comes from a Hebrew word - "avon" - which means - moral perversity, fault, mischief. Jesus took all our moral faults and offers to us deliverance and freedom. Many people struggle with things that they can not be set free from like addictions and re-occurring behaviour patterns but Jesus came to set the captives free. In Jesus there is hope of freedom.

John 8 v 36 "if the Son sets you free, you will be free indeed"

Free indeed means no turning back, not just a temporal freedom, but free forever to live and be who God created you to be.

Revelation 1 v 5 "To him who loved us and has freed us from our sins by his blood".

I believe that there is a difference between being forgiven for our sins and being set free from our sins. You can be forgiven but never be set free. There are some people who are always coming back to God every week to ask for forgiveness for the same sins because they are being forgiven but they are not being set free. We need to get a revelation that Jesus has not only made provision for us to be forgiven but he has made provision for us to be set free which is far greater.

John 8 v 32 "You will know the truth and the truth will set you free".

Many are not set free because they have not got a revelation of the truth of the word and the truth of the finished work of the cross. The devil has kept them in ignorance that the price has been paid for them to be completely healed and set free. The bible says that people are destroyed because of a lack of knowledge. We need to get a revelation of the truth of all that God has purchased for us and to receive our deliverance and freedom by faith. It is for freedom that Christ has set us free

Galatians 5 v 1 "stand firm then and do not let yourselves be burdened again by a yoke of slavery.

Once we have been set free we also need to stand and walk in our freedom and not allow ourselves to slip back into our old ways again. We need to know that in Christ we are a new creation and the old has gone and the new has come (2 Cor 5 v 17).

V 5 "by his wounds you are healed".

Every wound that Jesus took on his back was for our healing - when they flogged Jesus, it was for our healing. He took every sickness in his body and exchanges back to us total healing and restoration. Through the cross, we can partake of the divine nature (2 Peter 1 v 4) and as we looked at earlier, God can not be sick, it is not in his nature to be sick so if we are partaking of the divine nature, then we also should not be sick. He took our sickness and exchanges back to us healing and restoration.

The word "healed" comes from a Hebrew word - "Rapha" and it means -to make whole, to mend (by stitching), repair. The concept of mend by stitching is an interesting one. It reminds me of Isaiah 6 when Isaiah met the Lord and he said "Woe is me I am un-done" (KJV). Sometimes we are un-done and we have had the stuffing knocked out of us by the things of life and we need to be sewn up again and restored and renewed.

In Mathew 8 v 16-18 when Jesus was healing the sick and casting out demons it says in v 17 "this was to fulfil what was spoken through the prophet Isaiah "he took up our infirmities and carried our diseases". Everywhere that Jesus went, people were healed and set free just by a word, just by a touch, just by his presence. He was confirming the word that the Messiah himself would come to heal and restore the people. When he walked on the earth he healed <u>all</u> who came to him and through the cross he has made provision for all who come to him to still be healed and to walk in health. At the cross a great divine exchange took place, he took all our rottenness and transferred back to us his divine nature and his divine blessings.

Recently at a mission in India, there was a lady who came forward to testify that the Lord had restored her eye sight. In order to check out what she could see, I asked her what was on the sign at the back of the platform. In our country, we might ask someone to read something but I have discovered that in some rural villages most people are not able to read so instead I may ask them to describe something. So, I asked this lady to describe what was on the banner hanging on the platform and she replied "The Cross". Her answer summed up everything - she could see the cross and the reason that she was now able to see the cross was because of the cross!! Jesus had healed and restored her eye sight because of the finished work on the cross. I then declared to the people listening - "this lady can now see because of the cross". I encourage you today, that all that we need has already been done - all we have to do is reach out and receive it by faith.

The Divine Exchange

He was wounded, so that we can be healed - 1 Peter 2 v 24
He was made sin, so that we can be righteous - 2 Corinthians 5 v 21
He experienced death, so that we can receive life - Romans 6 v 23
He became poor, so that we can receive riches - 2 Corinthians 8 v 9
He bore our shame, so that we can share his glory - Hebrews 12 v 2

He took our rejection, so that we can be accepted - Ephesians 1 v 5-6

He became a curse, so that we can inherit a blessing - Galatians 3 v 13-14

Today I want you to see that the price for your healing has been paid and all that you have to do is reach out in faith and receive it.

CHAPTER 3

The Ministry of Jesus

Acts 10 v 38 "God anointed Jesus of Nazareth with the Holy Spirit and power and how he went around doing good and healing all who were under the power of the devil because God was with him".

I love the word <u>all</u> - Jesus did not decide to just heal a few select favourites but he healed <u>all</u> who came to him. Many times people will say that Jesus did not heal everyone and so therefore he does not heal every one today. It is true that Jesus did not heal everyone but from my reading of scripture, it appears that he healed every one who actually came to him and asked him to heal them. I don't read anywhere in the bible where someone came to Jesus and he told them to go away.

Mathew 14 v 35-36 "When the men of that place recognised Jesus, they sent word to all the surrounding country. People brought all their sick to him and begged him to let the sick just touch the edge of his cloak, and <u>all</u> who touched him were healed.

Mathew 9 v 35 "Jesus went through all the towns and synagogues preaching the good news of the Kingdom and healing <u>every</u> disease and sickness"

When Jesus says "every", then he means "every". Let me encourage you today that there is not one single sickness that

Jesus is not able to heal and there is not one single sickness that he has not made provision for on the cross. In v 36 it says that he saw the crowds being harassed and he had compassion on them. When Jesus looks and sees his people who he died for in pain, then he has compassion on them and desires to see them well.

Mathew 10 v 1 "He called his twelve disciples to him and gave them authority to drive out evil spirits and to heal every disease and sickness".

Here he called his disciples and sent them out with his authority to heal every disease and sickness. As we will look at later, not only does Jesus want to heal us but he has also given us power and authority to go in his name and heal others.

Mathew 8 v 16 "he drove out the spirits with a word and healed all the sick.

Even when he cast out demons it says he cast them out with a word - one single word and the demons left - what do you think that word was? Maybe it was simply "GO", or "OUT". How often do we complicate things in long drawn out sessions, when if we are truly walking in power and authority, we can simply command and sickness will obey us and leave. Jesus gave the same authority in his name to his disciples and we should be continuing on the healing ministry of Jesus as we will look at later in the book.

Jesus treated sickness as an enemy

It is interesting to note how Jesus confronted sickness - in Luke 4 v 38-39 it says that Simon's mother in law was suffering from a fever and when Jesus saw her "he rebuked the fever" and it left her. The word rebuke is a harsh stern word and it can only be used by someone who is in a position of authority against someone who has done something wrong. When Jesus saw this lady suffering with a fever, he took authority over the fever, he spoke harshly to it and commanded it to leave and it did leave.

The word "rebuke" comes from a Greek word "epitimao" and one of the meanings of that is - to forbid. Jesus forbids sickness to be in a child of God, it is not allowed to be there - it is a trespasser that must be evicted!

This tells us several things; number one, it tells us that Jesus does not like sickness and that it has nothing to do with him; it does not originate with him but with the devil. It tells us that when he sees his children being sick, it upsets him and makes him angry and thirdly it tells us that he has all power and authority to rebuke it and make it go away. In v 39 it says that she got up <u>at once</u> and began to wait on them. The minute that Jesus spoke and then touched her, the fever had to leave. There are many ways that Jesus ministered healing in the bible; sometimes he laid hands on people, sometimes he just touched them, sometimes he spoke the word either to them or even from a distance, sometimes it was the faith of friends and sometimes he did even stranger things than that as we may look at later;

but the end result was that they were <u>all</u> healed.

In Luke 13 v10-16 we read the story of a lady who was crippled and bent over and could not straighten up at all. When Jesus saw her he called out to her "woman, you are set free from your infirmity". Then he put his hands on her and <u>immediately</u> she straightened up and praised God. It is interesting to note that in v 11, it says that this woman had been crippled by a spirit for eighteen years. What kind of spirit was this talking about? It was certainly not God's spirit; it was a demonic spirit that had been binding her all those years. When the religious people began to moan about Jesus healing on the wrong day again, he replies to them;

v 16 "Then should not this woman, a daughter of Abraham whom satan has kept bound for eighteen long years, be set free on the Sabbath day from what bound her?".

Here Jesus makes no illusion as to who the source of her condition was; it was the devil who had made her crippled all those years and it was Jesus who had come to set her free with just one word and one touch! There can be many people who are crippled not just physically but also emotionally and it causes them to not be able to walk uprightly with God and they live their lives bowed down in shame and un-worthiness but Jesus came to lift up our heads and set us free.

In Mathew 12 v 22 the people brought a demon possessed man to Jesus who was blind and mute. When Jesus prayed for him he was totally healed and could see and speak. To begin with the crowds were amazed but then the religious people began to say that he was only using demonic powers to cast out demons. In v 25 Jesus knew their thoughts and he tells them "every kingdom divided against itself will be ruined". He then rebukes the people for blasphemy against the Holy Spirit. Jesus knew that it was the devil who had bound this man and he was coming in power and authority to set him free. Jesus did not use big long prayers when he healed the sick, he simply spoke the word and commanded the sicknesses to leave because he knew who he was and the authority that he carried. Therefore from these examples and many more we can see that Jesus always saw sickness as an enemy; a trespasser in someone's lives that should be removed immediately.

God's Willingness

There was a leper who came to Jesus in Luke 5 v 12-13 and he came hesitantly because he knew that Jesus was able to heal him if he wanted to but he was afraid of his willingness to do it for him. Most of us would say that God could heal us if he wanted to because we believe that God has power to do whatever he wants to do. But the problem comes in our minds with "will he do it for me?". Sometimes this can be the result of either wrong teaching or a wrong image of ourselves, maybe we don't feel worthy to ask God for anything. But when we get a revelation that it is not about being worthy - none of us are worthy in our own abilities but through the cross Jesus has taken all our sicknesses and the price for our healing has already been paid. Therefore it is not a case of whether Jesus is going to heal us or not - the truth is that he has already healed us over 2,000 years ago. What we are doing is believing that and reaching out to receive what has already been done. The leper had this problem of God's willingness but Jesus said to him in v 13 "I am willing, be clean" and immediately he was healed. I like that word <u>immediately</u>. When Jesus touches you something will happen. I do believe that sometimes God can heal gradually and I have seen this happen, sometimes he uses a variety of different ways to bring about his healing but when I pray for someone I am always praying and believing for <u>immediately</u> to happen in that persons life. When Jesus shows up in your life and situation then something will happen - just one touch from the King changes everything! There are times when God will use a combination of both medical things and prayer but at other times there is a divine miracle that only God could have done - those are the most glorious times and no one can deny that God has done a great work.

As I have travelled around the world I have seen great miracles and sometimes we think that God does more miracles abroad in places like Africa and India etc but I believe that God is the same everywhere, it is only people's expectation levels that can change. God responds to faith and where faith is then he will move and the people will receive. I also think that our dependence is different according to where we live; for example in India recently I saw a lot of older people having their eye sight restored; whereas in this country, as long as people had their glasses on and were able to see, they probably wouldn't even think of praying for that as a healing need. But in those countries, a lot of the people are so poor that they can not afford to and go some prescription glasses to wear so they have a need to be healed and God heals them. So the first thing that we need to understand is that Jesus is willing to heal us because he has already made provision for that healing on the cross. There is no healing that is big or small, I have come to realise that anything that is a concern for you is a concern to God because he loves you.

Healing on the Sabbath

In Mathew 12 v 9-14 the religious people were looking for a way to accuse Jesus and wanted to catch him out healing on the Sabbath day. There was a man there with a shrivelled hand and Jesus tells him to stretch out his hand and it was restored. Then he turns to the religious people and begins to give an illustration asking them what they would do if one of their animals fell into the pit on the Sabbath - would they leave it there until the next day or would they immediately pull it out. If they had that much concern for an injured animal, then how much more Jesus has compassion on his children and wants them to be well. Jesus is not so much concerned with rules and regulations as he is with love and compassion to heal his people. That man went on his way rejoicing and was totally healed because he had met Jesus that day. Every one who met Jesus was completely changed and it is still happening today. There are some people who want to tell you that miracles are not for today but the bible says that Jesus Christ is the same, yesterday, today and forever. Nearly every page that you turn in the gospels you will find Jesus healing someone or setting someone free and totally changing lives and he is still the same today.

It is God's will to heal you

Sometimes people struggle with - is it God's will to heal me?

John 5 v 19 "I tell you the truth, the Son can do nothing by himself; he can only do what he sees his Father doing, because whatever the Father does, the Son does also".

John 6 v 38 "For I have come down from heaven not to do my will but to do the will of him who sent me".

Here we see that Jesus came to do the will of the Father and that he only did what he saw the Father telling him to do. So what did Jesus do while he was on earth? He went around preaching and healing the sick. Therefore it must be the will of the Father to heal people.

The Faith of Friends

In Luke 4 v 40-41 it says that as the sun was setting people brought to Jesus all who had various sicknesses and he healed them. Such was the fame of Jesus around the towns, that people's faith level was rising to the point where they literally brought their sick people for Jesus to lay his hands on them.

Luke 5 v 17 "And the power of the Lord was present for him to heal the sick.

There was a special meeting that was taking place and many miracles were happening. Then in Luke 5 v 18-19 it says that some friends came carrying a paralysed man on a mat and tried to bring him to Jesus but because of the crowd they could not find a way to get into the house where Jesus was, so they went up on the roof and took the tiles away and lowered the man down right in front of Jesus! What a story of faith and persistence - how many of us would have decided to go home and try again another day? But these friends were not going to let the miracle for their friend pass by - they were willing to go up on the roof. In v 20 it says when "Jesus saw their faith". He saw the faith of the friends and what they were doing. Sometimes we need friends to bring us to Jesus, sometimes we need friends who will pray for us and believe for us because when we are feeling ill, it can be hard to believe for ourselves. We can become disappointed and find it hard to hold on to faith and in those times we need friends who are willing to raise the roof for us! Jesus spoke to the man and said "friend, your sins are forgiven". How interesting that the man came paralysed and needing healing and yet Jesus speaks about his sins being forgiven. Sometimes we think that we need physical healing but there is actually a much greater need first. It is interesting that Jesus calls him "friend". When we come to Jesus, his greatest desire is to call us into a relationship with him. We can get into heaven with a sick body but we can't get into heaven with a sick spirit - but as the man received the forgiveness, he was also completely healed and he picked up his mat and went home rejoicing.

Jesus came to restore body, soul and spirit and that day the paralysed man received salvation in its totality - forgiveness for his sins and healing for his body. In v 26 all the people exclaimed "we have seen remarkable things today"! I want to tell you that in all the places that I am going, I am seeing remarkable things - Jesus is still doing miracles today and he has one just for you too!

Never give up when Jesus is in town

The Woman with the issue of blood

One of the most famous stories in the bible concerning healing is the woman with the issue of blood. In this instance, it was an issue of blood, but there can be many issues that we need Jesus to touch in our lives.

Luke 8 v 43 "And a woman was there who had been subject to bleeding for twelve years but no-one could heal her".

Here was a woman who had been bleeding for 12 years and no one could heal her.

Luke 8 v 44 "She came up behind him and touched the edge of his cloak, and immediately her bleeding stopped".

Twelve years of pain and suffering ended that day because she just touched Jesus. This was a woman who was determined to get a miracle despite all the opposition around her. Not only was she sick, but she would have been considered an out-cast and un-clean because of her bleeding - she should not have even been in the crowd but she was determined to push through to get her miracle. She could have given up because there was a large crowd and it was hard to get near to Jesus; maybe many people had shunned her and told her to go away and yet she refused to go away. She had determined in her heart that she was going to touch Jesus. In fact, she even delayed him from going to Jarius's daughter who was dying. She dared to interrupt Jesus in the midst of another mission! As she reached out to him; Jesus said "who touched me?" (v 45) . His disciples thought he was being crazy because there was such a large crowd that many people were touching him; but Jesus recognised the touch of faith; he knew that someone had touched him because power had gone out from him. When the woman saw that she could not go un-noticed, she came trembling at his feet and told him what she had done. I wonder what she expected him to say? But Jesus simply says to her "daughter, your faith has healed you, go in peace" (v 48). There are several things in that one sentence; first of all he offers her acceptance by calling her "daughter", not only was she healed physically but she was received into the family of God that day and then he tells her to go in peace. I wonder if up until that day, she had any peace in her life? But that day, she left feeling loved, accepted, totally healed and with peace restored in her life - what a day! Afterwards Jesus calmly goes on his way to now raise Jarius's daughter from the dead who has now died while he was delayed with the lady with the issue of blood! When all hope is gone, Jesus turns up. The people from the house of Jarius come running out of the house to tell Jesus to not bother any more because the girl has now died - it is too late! But Jesus simply tells them to believe and then proceeds to raise her up again bringing hope and joy to another family.

Blind Bartimeus

In Mark 10 v 46-52 there was a man who was blind and he was sitting by the roadside begging when suddenly he heard a commotion going on around him and he knew that Jesus was passing by. Maybe this man had sat by the road side for many years begging and seeing no hope for his life but this day was a different day, this day was his day for a miracle, he would never be the same again. As he hears Jesus approaching, he begins to shout out "Jesus, Son of David, have mercy on me". The crowds around him told him to shut up and to be quiet; but he refused to be quiet. Sometimes in our own lives, there will be people who want to tell us to give up our faith, don't bother crying out to Jesus. Maybe we have been in a meeting and when the call has come to go to the front for prayer, we have held back because we are afraid of what people will think of us, we feel embarrassed and self conscious but this man was not going to let intimidation hold him back from receiving his miracle; so he shouted all the louder until he got the attention of Jesus. In v 49 it says that Jesus stopped. Up until that point, Jesus was not looking at him; he had no intention of healing him that day; until he heard his cry. I believe that there is a lesson in this for us. I have heard many people say "well, if Jesus wants to heal me; then he will". But the principle here is that Jesus was passing by, he was walking in the crowd and would have passed by that blind man until he heard him shouting out. Sometimes we have to call out. Suddenly the attitude of the crowd changes towards the man and now they are telling him "cheer up, on your feet, he's calling you"!

Then the blind man does an interesting and amazing act of faith - in v 50 it says "throwing his cloak aside, he jumped to his feet and came to Jesus". He threw his cloak aside when he heard Jesus calling him. The cloak that he was wearing would have been a beggars cloak, it would have told people that he was blind; but the minute that he heard the voice of Jesus calling him; faith rose up inside of him and he knew - I don't need this beggars cloak anymore - he knew he was going to be healed. When he came to Jesus, then Jesus asks him "what do you want me to do for you?". The man was blind and yet Jesus still asks him "what do you want?". This again shows us the principle that Jesus will never assume what we want even if it looks obvious, we have to ask. We might assume that if someone is blind, then obviously they want to see; but actually I have had blind people come to me for prayer and say that they would like emotional healing in their lives and they do not even ask for prayer for physical healing. Therefore often we will find that Jesus asked people what they wanted. The blind man said "Rabbi, I want to see" and Jesus says to him "Go, your faith has healed you". It was his faith that had healed him - faith to cry out when everyone around told him to be quiet, faith to throw off his cloak when he heard the voice of Jesus calling his name, faith to come and ask to be healed. That day his life was changed forever - no longer blind - no longer a beggar and all because he had decided in his heart that he would not let Jesus pass by.

Lazarus

John 11 v 38 "Jesus, once more deeply moved, came to the tomb. It was a cave with a stone laid across the entrance. Take away the stone, he said. But Lord said Martha, the sister of the dead man, by this time there is a bad odour, for he has been there four days".

Here one of Jesus' friends had died. His sisters, Mary and Martha had called for Jesus when he was ill, but he did not make it before Lazarus died.

V 32 "Lord if you had been here, my brother would not have died"

Mary was asking Jesus "why did you not come earlier? Now it is too late!". Sometimes we feel that Jesus is too late in our situations. But Jesus had a plan as to what he was going to do. The sisters thought it was too late, but it is never too late for Jesus - he always has a plan. When they get to the tomb, he tells them to take away the stone. They are reluctant to do so, because they can not see the point and anyway there will be a bad smell for he has been dead for four days. Sometimes we have stones that have to be removed before we can see the glory of God. Only they could remove the stone - Jesus did not pray until they had removed the stone themselves. Maybe our stones are un-belief, disappointment, apathy, un-forgiveness, wrong teaching. Whatever our stone is; Jesus says that if you remove it; you will see the glory of God.

V 40 "Did I not tell you that if you believed, you would see the glory of God".

Jesus is trying to tell them, that he is going to do a miracle if they will believe. As they take away the stone, Jesus looks up to heaven and prays and he calls out;

V 43 "Lazarus Come out!"
V 44 "The dead man came out, his hands and feet wrapped with strips of linen, and a cloth around his face. Jesus said to them. Take off the grave clothes and let him go".

When Jesus called his name, resurrection life came and he was raised from the dead. The day of mourning became a day of celebration. It is interesting that Jesus tells the sisters to take off the grave clothes. Lazarus came out still bound and un-able to move. I believe that this represents the emotional baggage in our lives - we can receive physical healing but sometimes we are still walking around with grave clothes on and unable to walk properly before God. Jesus told the sisters to take them off. In the body of Christ, we are called to take the grave clothes off other people and bring healing to them so they can be free.
Be encouraged today, that when all hope is gone; Jesus turns up.

According to your faith

In Mathew 9 v 27-30 there were 2 blind men who were following Jesus and asking him to heal them and he says to them "Do you believe that I am able to do this" and when they say "yes Lord", then he replies "according to your faith will it be done to you" and their sight was restored. Many times Jesus asked people - "what do you want? - do you want to get well?, do you believe that I am able to do this?". We see that faith is very much linked with receiving our healing - we have to believe in order to receive.

In Mark 9 v 17-27 there was a man who had brought his son who was possessed by an evil spirit to the disciples for them to cast it out. This spirit threw the boy into convulsions and caused him to be deaf and mute. When the disciples were unable to cast out the spirit, they brought the boy to Jesus and the boy's father says to Jesus "if you can do anything". Jesus replies by saying "everything is possible for him who believes" and at once the man exclaims " I do believe, help me overcome my unbelief". He believed that Jesus could do something but he had doubts as to whether he would for him just like the leper did. Most of us believe that God can do something but sometimes we struggle with those nagging doubts in our minds. Jesus had compassion on the man and his son and cast the spirit out and he was completely healed and restored. God knows our hearts and if we are standing in as much faith as we have at the time, he will make up for the rest. Faith is the total opposite of our natural thinking. We say that when we see it then we will believe it; but God says; believe it first by faith and then you will see it manifested in your life. This principle works not only for healing but for anything that we are praying and believing God for. We have to see it by faith first and then we wait for it to be manifested in the natural realm.

How do we get faith? The bible says that Faith comes by hearing and hearing by the word of God (Romans 10 v 17) so as we read the word and see how Jesus healed other people and as we allow his word to become real in our lives, then faith will begin to rise up inside of us. We can also get faith by listening to testimonies of what has happened to other people and think; "if that can happen to them, then it can happen to me too". The more time that we spend in prayer and the presence of God, then faith begins to rise within us; as we are in an anointed meeting, then faith begins to rise up within us - there is an atmosphere for miracles present. Many times I have been in a meeting where I have seen faith on people and I know that they are ready to receive their healing. Often I will then pray for those people first and as they are healed then faith rises in all the other people who are also waiting to receive. Even if we have faith as small as a mustard seed, we can make it grow.

I do not however, believe in condemning people for not having enough faith or tell people that the reason they are not healed is because of not having enough faith. I have known many people with great faith and some are healed and some are not and as I said at the beginning of the book, I don't claim to have all the answers but all I know is that the more we proclaim the truth and pray for people, I believe that more and more people will be healed. If you have had great faith and you are still waiting for your miracle, I want to encourage you to not grow weary and lose heart for God has a plan for your life and it is a good plan.

Do you Want to Get Well

In Luke 5 v 1-9 we read the story about a man who had been an invalid for 38 years and every day he came to sit by the pool of Bethesda. Many disabled people used to come there every day because they thought that the water had healing properties. The first person to get into the water was thought to be healed when the angel stirred the waters and every day these people came looking for a miracle. This man had sat there day after day but because he was so disabled, he was never able to get into the water before someone else made it there before him. How amazing that in Jesus there is healing for all who will come; we are not waiting in a queue. Some people think that God's power is limited but he is limitless. I have even had some people say to me "Oh, I didn't bother coming up with my small need for healing as I could see that there were people with much greater needs than mine". Almost as if, if God healed them, then he would not have as much power left to heal a more serious condition! God has enough for all! Jesus speaks to this man by the pool and in v 6 he asks him "do you want to get well?". We may think that was a strange question to ask because surely he wanted to get well. But I have known many people who are not sure if they really want to get well. Sometimes people have got used to the lifestyle of being sick; they have got used to the attention that they get or the benefits that they receive and they are in-secure to step into the un-known of being healthy especially, if like this man; it has been a long standing illness in their lives and maybe they have never known much else. Suddenly if they were healed; what would they do; what would their life be like? Therefore like anything that we receive from God, we have to ask, we will not just receive without asking in faith and wanting to be healed. In v 7 this man gives a big list of reasons why he has not been healed but Jesus simply says to him "pick up your mat and walk" With those words, the man picked up his mat and was completely healed.

Today Jesus is asking you "do you want to get well"?

Gradual or instant healing

Most of the places in the bible where Jesus healed people, it was <u>immediately</u> and I believe that this is what we need to seek for. But occasionally there is a gradual healing that takes places; almost as if God just speeds up the healing process. Maybe it can be "according to our faith". If we have faith for instant, then we can receive instant but if we believe that God will simply help us to get better gradually, then our faith is at that level to receive.

The 10 Lepers

In Luke 17 v 11-19 we read the story of the 10 men who were cleansed of leprosy. All ten men came to Jesus asking for help and in v 14 he tells them to go and show themselves to the priest and "as they went, they were cleansed". In Leviticus 14 v 2-3 when a person had an infectious skin disease and thought that he had been healed, he had to go to the priest to be examined to see if he was completely cleansed and could enter back into the main stream of society again. A person with leprosy was considered un-clean and cast out from the assembly of the Lord. Therefore when Jesus told them to go and show themselves to the priests, he was telling them that they were healed but their act of faith was that they had to go to the priest by faith - and as they went, they were healed. Was their healing noticeable at the moment that Jesus spoke? Or did their healing become more noticeable the nearer that they got to the priest? We are not told, we can only put our own thoughts on it, but the healing was done the moment that Jesus spoke, but maybe it took a few minutes/hours for the healing to become noticeable in the natural realm. They could have stood there and said "but how can we go to the priest, when we are still leprous?". The truth for us, is that we are healed because the word has healed us - the cross has healed us - the work is already finished but our faith has to see it in order for it to manifest in the natural realm.

I prayed for a lady once in a meeting who had serious back pain and at the time she told me that she noticed no difference in the pain. I remember that I was feeling quite disappointed as this lady had come in faith believing to be healed and yet she left feeling the same. However this same lady phoned me up a week later to tell me that when she got in the car to drive home, suddenly all the pain left! This is what I have come to call the "instant delayed healing". It was instant when it happened, it was not a gradual healing but it was just delayed by a few minutes! I do not know why this happens but I now encourage people that even if they do not feel healed when they leave a meeting, that they should not allow discouragement to come because they may find that even as they go home or even as they wake up the next morning, that they will find that they are now healed. Sometimes we do not understand all that goes on in the heavenly realms and maybe there is a battle that is going on for the manifestation to take place or maybe sometimes God does it so that only he gets the glory. I do believe though that we should always pray believing for an instant miracle as this is encouraging for the person and it is also a testimony to the other people in the meeting.

Even Jesus had to pray twice sometimes

Often we think that it is a lack of faith to pray again if we are not healed the first time BUT; even Jesus had to pray more than once on occasions.

Mark 8 v 22-25 Jesus prayed for a man who was blind and after he had spat on the man's eyes and put his hands on him; he asks him "do you see anything?" and he replies "I see people, they look like trees walking around". In other words, he had received a measure of healing but his vision was still blurred, it was not complete. Therefore Jesus put his hands on his eyes once more and this time his sight was completely restored.

If you are in a meeting and someone prays for you, don't be afraid to say if there is still some pain there, because if you don't say anything, then you may leave with half your healing instead of the total restoration. I will often ask "now, how many people here feel something has changed, but it is not complete yet?" Then if people raise their hands, I will call them forward because I believe that God does not do half a job, he wants completion and most of the time as I then pray a second time for those people, then they are healed. Often faith is also at a higher level at that point as I am believing that if God has begun a measure of healing, then he will bring it to completion and the people themselves have already seen something happen so they are also believing for the total healing to take place.

Now there are some people who deny facts and because they believe they are standing in faith; they will not even acknowledge that they are sick. I do not believe that God calls us to deny facts; if we don't feel well, then that is a fact but it is not the truth. What we are called to do is acknowledge our need; but then speak the truth of the word into the need. If we are never acknowledging that we have a problem then we can not come to the Lord for an answer. So if you have a bad stomach, then you may have pain and feel un-well, that is a fact; but then you begin to speak to your stomach and tell it that Jesus has taken this sickness on the cross and that by his wounds you are healed. Then by faith you believe that his word will begin to change the facts so that your body lines up with the truth.

Do something by Faith

After we have received prayer, then we need to do something by faith. We saw in one of the previous stories that Jesus told the man with the shrivelled hand "to stretch it out" and as he did so, it was healed. Often after I have prayed for people, I will then ask them to do something that they couldn't do before to test out their healing. For example, if they had a bad back, then I might ask them to bend down, or if they had a stiff shoulder, then I will ask them to raise their arm up as far as it will go. Often as they do this, they receive the fullness of their healing. If the person was unable to walk very well, then I will ask them to walk around the room. I remember one lady in Kenya who was in a lot of pain in her legs and had to sit throughout the ministry time because it was too painful to stand up, but as I prayed for her to be healed; she found that the pain had gone and she ended up dancing with me on the platform! Praise God!

Acts 3 v 7 "Taking him by the right hand, he helped him up and instantly the man's feet and ankles became strong. He jumped to his feet and began to walk".

Here Peter and John had prayed for a lame man at the gate Beautiful and after speaking healing to him, then they took a hold of his hand and helped him to get up. He had to receive his healing by doing something by faith. When we receive healing, we have to walk in our healing and do something by faith that we couldn't do before.

Thankfulness

In this story of the ten lepers, only one of them came back to say thank you to Jesus.

Luke 17 v 17 "Were not all ten cleansed?, where are the other nine?".

When we receive our healing, we need to make sure that we are thankful to the one who has healed us and give him praise. Many come to Jesus only for what they can receive but then they continue with their own lives not giving glory to the Lord who has saved them. In v 19 Jesus speaks to this one man and says "Rise and go, your faith has made you well". The other 9 were cleansed but this one was made well. We can receive physical healing but only by worshipping God with our whole lives, will we be totally whole and restored. This man was made totally whole in every way and went on his way rejoicing. As well as giving thanks to God, it is also good to give testimony and also to let the person who prayed for us know what has happened. Sometimes I find that I find out many years later what has happened to someone and that is ok as Jesus is the one who is the healer and I am just the vessel but sometimes it is good for people to know what has happened as it is encouraging to see what God is doing and it can help others who are going through a similar situation.

CHAPTER 4

MISUNDERSTANDINGS ABOUT HEALING

I am sure that many of us have heard different reasons as to why people are not healed but most of them are probably not even scriptural and I want us to look at some of these misunderstandings now. The bible says that "my people are destroyed from lack of knowledge" (Hosea 4 v 6). When we don't understand what the word of God says, then the enemy can steal our blessings from us. I believe that there are many lies that the enemy has tried to speak into our lives to make us accept sickness.

1. <u>God made you sick to teach you something</u>

Sometimes, we feel that God has made us sick to punish us or to teach us a lesson. Firstly we need to understand that God is our father and as a perfect heavenly father, he does not desire for his children to be sick and he does not use sickness as a punishment. 2 Timothy 2 v 16 "all scripture is God breathed and is useful for teaching, rebuking and correcting". So it is scripture that is used for correcting, not sickness. How many of you who are parents would wish for your children to be sick if they were going astray so that they might learn a lesson? None of you, I hope! If we would not wish that upon our own children, then how much more does God not wish that for his own children whom he has laid down his life for on the cross.

Secondly, we need to understand that sickness does not

originate with God, he is not the author of sickness. Sickness did come as a result of original sin in the garden because it was then that our bodies became corruptible and death entered in; but God did not create sickness, it was from the devil and a result of man's original sin. If we have been living in open sin (I am not talking about making a few mistakes, which we all do) then sometimes the enemy may have taken advantage of an open door in our lives, when we walked out of the protection of God in order to be able to attack us with sickness. So, we may need to repent of our sin first before asking the Lord to heal us. Remember also that repent means to "turn away", so we must have a total change of heart and lifestyle, not just "I am sorry" but then continue the same.

In Luke 5 where Jesus healed the man at the pool, he found him again later on and in v 14 he says to him "see you are well again, stop sinning or something worse may happen to you". Obviously this man was doing something that was not pleasing to the Lord and the Lord was warning him that he had now received his healing and that he should change his lifestyle to worship God or else he may lose his healing.

Many times when Jesus healed people he told them that their sins were forgiven almost as if that was the root cause of their sickness. In the Old Testament it did seem as if God allowed sickness to come upon people for disobedience but now we are under New Testament covenant of the cross where all sickness has been taken; therefore God will not bring sickness to anyone; so God did not make you sick but if you realise that you have been in sin, then maybe the enemy was allowed to attack you, but if you repent then God will restore you.

2. This sickness is to glorify God

First of all, let me say that God is not glorified by something that he came to destroy! Acts 10 v 38 "he went around doing good and healing all who were under the power of the devil". Jesus came to destroy sickness and set people free. He is glorified by healing, not by sickness.

Sometimes where we make a mistake is because we see God bringing good out of a time of sickness and so we believe that God caused it for his glory. Every situation that we go through in life, God will use and bring good out of it if we allow him to; but that does not mean that he caused every situation; it just means that he can use it if we will allow him to.

For example if we have been in hospital and then we were able to speak to someone about the Lord, we may think that God sent us to hospital so that someone could be spoken to, but the reality is that God was simply bringing something good out of a bad situation.

3. This is my cross that I have to bear

Again this is a misunderstanding of the word of God when we hear people saying that the sickness that they have is their cross that they have to bear. Jesus did say that we were to take up our cross and follow him but this has nothing to do with sickness and more to do with giving our whole lives to the service of God. Let me tell you, that there was only one cross and Jesus has already hung on it and taken all of our sins and sicknesses and by his wounds we are healed. If our sicknesses have already been taken, then why are we needing to carry them again? If we went to a restaurant and someone else paid for the bill, what would we do? Would we think "well, I can't believe that the bill has been paid, let me go and pay again"!! How ridiculous and how insulting to the one who has offered to pay for you. When we want to think that we are carrying our cross of sickness for God's glory then we are denying the work of the cross that has already been done. Instead let us say thank you and accept the gift that has been purchased for us.

4. God will heal me in his time

This is one that I have heard people say many times; God will heal me when he is ready to do so. Let me tell you that Jesus has already healed you over 2,000 years ago - it is a finished work at the cross. Therefore all we have to do is to believe that and to receive it by faith. We are not waiting for God to do something, he has already done it - he is not going to do anything else; but we are going to reach out and receive the gift of healing that has already been paid for.

5. God will heal me if he wants to

Sometimes we may have been taught that it is not God's will to always heal people. I want you to think about what we pray in the Lord's prayer - "thy will be done, on earth, as it is in heaven". We are praying for God's will in heaven to be manifested on the earth. So let me ask you a question; do you believe that there is any sickness in heaven? Most people would not believe that there is any sickness in heaven and some people are just waiting to get to heaven so they can be healed. Of course we will be totally healed with no more pain when we get to heaven, but through the cross there is provision for us to live in health here on earth and when we pray the Lord's prayer we are praying for what is in heaven to be manifested here on earth. Healing is in heaven and we are calling it here on earth through faith. We have already established that the work has been done on the cross. Just like the leper who came to Jesus and said "Lord if you are willing, you can make me clean". Jesus said to him "I am willing, be clean". Today Jesus is willing to heal you and the provision has already been made on the cross - today you can reach out in faith and receive all that has been purchased for you. His will in heaven is waiting to be manifested on earth.

6. <u>What about Paul's thorn in the flesh?</u>

Many people talk about Paul's thorn in the flesh and that he pleaded with God to take it away and that God refused to do so. Let us look at this passage of scripture and see what Paul's thorn in the flesh could have actually been referring to. In 2 Corinthians 12 v 7 it says "to keep me from becoming conceited because of these surpassingly great revelations, there was given me a thorn in my flesh, a messenger of satan to torment me. Three times I pleaded with the Lord to take it away from me, but he said to me, my grace is sufficient for you".

First of all, the thorn came because of great revelations that Paul was having. Some people who want to claim they have a thorn in the flesh, never have any revelations! Secondly we can see that the thorn had nothing to do with God, it was a messenger of satan to torment him. Thirdly it does not say that the thorn was a sickness. If you read the preceding chapter you will see that Paul listed all of his hardships in ministry including persecutions, but he does not mention sickness.

In Numbers 33 v 55 and in Judges 2 v 3 it speaks of thorns in the flesh as being people who come to bring persecution to the people of God. Therefore I believe that Paul's thorn was persecution that he was experiencing for the sake of the gospel and God said to him that his grace was sufficient for him to stand up against it and endure. In Fact in v 10 of 2 Corinthians 12 it actually says "I delight in weaknesses, in insults, in hardships, in persecutions, in difficulties. For when I am weak, then I am strong". He does not list sickness and disease in this list. Therefore I do not believe that Paul's thorn was a sickness but was in fact persecution.

7. Miracles are not for today

I have heard many people say that miracles are not for today and that they ended after the early church died. I have heard some people quoting from this next passage;

1 Corinthians 13 v 8-10 "Love never fails. But where there are prophecies, they will cease; where there are tongues, they will be stilled; where there is knowledge it will pass away. For we

know in part and we prophesy in part, but when perfection comes, the imperfect disappears".

Has perfection come now? There is only one time when all things will be perfect and that is when Jesus comes again; so until then we are continuing on the work of the Lord and operating in all of the gifts of the Spirit that are available to us; which includes healing and miracles.

2 Corinthians 12 v 12 "The things that mark an apostle - signs, wonders and miracles"

Paul tells us that miracles are part of what make an apostle.

1 Corinthians 2 v 4 "My message and preaching were not with wise and persuasive words, but with a demonstration of the Spirit's power".

Miracles must follow the preaching of the word and even more so in these end times; they are a demonstration of the power of God to a lost world.

CHAPTER 5

DIFFERENT TYPES OF HEALING

The word "Rapha" means to make totally whole - nothing missing, nothing lacking. God has provided healing for the whole person. As well as normal healing, there are other types of healing that we can receive including creative miracles, emotional healing and deliverance.

Creative Miracles

Sometimes we need a physical healing, but sometimes we need a creative miracle. Some people have a problem with that; they believe that Jesus can heal but they doubt if he can replace a body part. I do not have any problem with believing this because if God could create us in the first place then it is not hard for him to replace a part if we need a new part during our life. I believe that there are angels who are waiting to bring new body parts down out of the storehouses of heaven when we pray. I prayed for a lady once who told me afterwards that she felt like God was giving her a whole new blood transfusion! There is nothing impossible for God.

John 9 v 1-11 we read the story of Jesus healing a man who was born blind but as you read this story, it becomes apparent that this may have been a creative miracle that took place. In v 6-7 it says that "he spat on the ground, made some mud with the saliva and put it on the man's eyes"

In the beginning man was created from the dust of the ground - we are clay with God's spirit breathed into us. Here Jesus made mud from the dust of the ground and put it on the man's eyes - I believe that he was actually creating new eyes - maybe the man was not just blind but he didn't even have any eyes at all - only sockets and Jesus created new eyes! When the man went to wash in the pool Siloam, he came home seeing. A creative miracle took place that day.

Inner Healing and Deliverance

Sometimes we need to be physically healed but sometimes we also need to be emotionally or mentally healed and often the two things can inter link together. If we carrying emotional burdens in our lives then it can often manifest itself into a physical condition as well. For example if we live our lives with anger and bitterness and un-forgiveness and disappointment then it is not surprising when we might develop arthritis or a heart condition because we are releasing the wrong kind of chemicals into our body through our wrong emotions. Many times it is essential to get to the root of a sickness with spiritual insight to get a total healing. Also we will see that when Jesus ministered to people, he would often go to the root of the situation.

Sometimes a sickness can also be caused by a demonic spirit attacking someone's life that needs to be cast out before healing can take place. As we said at the beginning, the source of all sickness is sin and the author of sickness is the devil; so it stands to reason that evil spirits will be involved in some sicknesses and diseases.

In Luke 13 we read the story of a lady who had been crippled by a spirit for 18 years. The bible says that she was bent over and could not straighten up at all. When Jesus saw her he said "woman, you are set free from your infirmity". She was obviously in a lot of pain, if she had not been able to straighten up for 18 years! Jesus identified that the source of her problem was a spirit of infirmity. There are some sicknesses that have a root of a spirit of infirmity that needs to be rebuked and cast out for the person to be free. Although this was a physical healing that took place, I believe that we can also interpret this story in an emotional way as well. There are many people who are crippled in an emotional way as well as physical. She was bent over and could not straighten up. Many people are bowed down with the cares of the world and the burdens that they are carrying to the extent that they are not able to walk properly with God.

Mathew 11 v 28 Jesus said "Come to me all you who are weary and burdened and I will give you rest".

Isaiah 61 v 1 "he has sent me to bind up the broken hearted, to proclaim freedom for the captives".
Isaiah 53 v 4 "he took up our infirmities and carried our sorrows"

Isaiah prophesied that one was coming who would preach good news, who would proclaim freedom to the captives and release the oppressed, the emotionally broken. He prophesied that on the cross, not only would the Messiah carry all our infirmities, but also our emotional sorrows. Then when Jesus came all those years later, he stood up in the synagogue and took the scroll of the prophet Isaiah and began reading from that very passage of scripture and then boldly declared to all those listening that he was the fulfilment of that prophecy.

Luke 4 v 21 "today this scripture is fulfilled in your hearing".

Therefore we see that Jesus came to not only heal physically but also emotionally.

Proverbs 13 v 12 says "hope deferred makes the heart sick". When we constantly have disappointments in our lives and people letting us down, it can cause us to become physically sick as well.

Proverbs 14 v 30 " a heart at peace gives life to the body, but envy rots the bones"

When we are at peace with God and with those around us, it gives life to our physical bodies, but if we live in envy and resentment it can rot the bones of our body. We can see how important it is to retain right attitudes in our emotions. Of course we will all go through times of disappointments and times where people let us down and times when people hurt us but we have to make a choice about what we do with those negative emotions. We need to decide to hand them over to the Lord and to allow his peace and healing to fill our lives rather than holding on to negative feelings that will ultimately destroy us. The peace of God is one of the most precious things that we can attain in life, it is something that money can not buy, it can not be earned, it is a gift of God but we have to be walking in a right relationship with God to attain the peace that passes all understanding. If we are living in disobedience or we are living in un-forgiveness or harbouring resentful feelings, then it will be very difficult for us to be experiencing the peace of God. When you have known the peace of God, you will not trade it for anything. Even in the midst of a storm, you can know the peace of God and it will strengthen and see you through. Peace in our hearts, gives life and balance to our whole bodies. When we are without peace, then there is turmoil and anxiety that occurs in our bodies leading to all kinds of illnesses including; high blood pressure, heart conditions, breathing problems, headaches, nervous conditions etc. Also if we are constantly anxious then we will probably have trouble sleeping which will cause our bodies to be tired leading to a lower immune system and making us more vulnerable to illnesses. As well as physical conditions, it will affect our relationships with people around us and so a vicious circle of events begins to take place in our lives in all areas.

Proverbs 15 v 30 "a cheerful look brings joy to the heart, and good news gives health to the bones".

There are many scriptures that make references to the bones. The bones are the very structure of our body. When the flesh has decayed, all that is left is the bones. When we are really cold, we will often remark that we are chilled to the bone - meaning that the cold has gone right to the very heart of us deep inside. When we harbour wrong emotions, it goes right to the very core of our being causing negative effects to take place in our body.

Proverbs 16 v 24 "pleasant words are a honeycomb, sweet to the soul and healing to the bones".

When we hear pleasant words, they are healing to our bones, our whole body. The bible says that life and death are in the power of the tongue. We can choose to speak life or death into ourselves and others with what we say. If we are still holding on to the memory of words spoken over us, then we need to take those to the Lord and ask him to break the power of the words that have been spoken. Sometimes people may have spoken negative things over us either knowingly in malice or innocently through ignorance. There is a famous saying "sticks and stones may break my bones, but words will never hurt me". Actually this is a totally wrong statement as words will often stay with us a lot longer in our memory than any physical hurt. Some people in their old age can still remember words that were spoken to them as a child and it is still affecting their lives as the wounds went deep. Some people were told that they were no good, that they were stupid etc and they have lived their whole life feeling in-adequate and always afraid to step out and do anything. Those words can become a burden that we carry until we ask the Lord to take them and set us free.

Proverbs 17 v 22 "a cheerful heart is good medicine, but a crushed spirit dries up the bones".

Being cheerful not only makes you feel better, but it is also good for your health. Even a doctor will tell you that you should laugh more. Laughter is good medicine for us - even God has a sense of humour. Much comedy today is unfortunately just in the form of rudeness but pure comedy is good for the soul and has healing in it. Let us decide today that we will find something to be cheerful about. Sometimes we naturally feel cheerful and at other times, we have to make a decision to be cheerful by an act of our will. There is a saying "smile and the whole world smiles with you". It is interesting today how very little people smile as they go through life. Today decide that whether you feel like it or not, that you will smile at someone - I guarantee that you will feel better afterwards and you may even get a smile back!

So, if you have been carrying emotional baggage in your life, then today decide that you are going to lay those things down at the foot of the cross and allow the healing power of God to flow into your life.

Demonic activity

Many times when Jesus ministered to people, he cast out different spirits including deaf spirits and mute spirits. Demonic spirits have to have been given an open door to have allowed them to enter in to someone's life and to be affecting them. Sometimes this can be the result of our own sin at some point in our lives but sometimes it can be a generational sin and we are suffering for things that our families were involved with in the past even up to several generations ago. If our families were involved with witchcraft or freemasonry or committed serious crimes, or were simply anti-God and living in rebellion to the ways of the Lord then the curses from these can still be running down our family line. Lines of addictions can also be passed down generational lines and curses of different sicknesses can also be followed in family lines. The truth is that all curses were broken at the cross (Galatians 3 v13-14) but we still have to come to a revelation of it in order to be set free. Many people are suffering innocently for things that they know nothing about.

Luke 11 v 14 "Jesus was driving out a demon that was mute. When the demon left the man could speak".

Here we see that the reason that this man could not speak was because a mute demon was binding his tongue. When we were in India recently there was a man who had been mute for the past 20 years and no-one in the village had heard him speaking. As we prayed for him and commanded his tongue to be released, he began to speak and came to the microphone to give his testimony - glory to God!

Another time in Mathew 17 v14-18 a man brought his son to Jesus for healing. The boy was suffering with seizures. In v 18 it says that "Jesus rebuked the demon and it came out of the boy, and he was healed from that moment".

There are many illnesses today which would resemble demonic activity and often people ask me about mental health problems and whether they are demonic. I believe that mental health is such a vast subject that I will not try to cover in this book, but I do believe that mental health is a complex issue and sometimes there can be more than one issue involved but definitely the enemy is involved in it somewhere as with all diseases. Often mental health illness can have a combination of emotional hurts in peoples lives and chemical imbalances in the brain as well as demonic activity. I believe that wherever there is a weakness, the enemy will always try to make it worse and so when he sees someone suffering with hurts and memories of the past, then he comes in with his lies to twist the mind further. It is interesting how when people describe hearing voices; the voices will always be negative, never positive. Often the voices will tell them to harm either themselves or someone else, so I definitely believe that the enemy is involved with mental health problems although it may not be the whole root. Often the root is rejection and hurts which have built up over time or it can be a result of an inherited disorder or it can be as a result of alcohol or drug misuse which has affected the brain. I have also seen that if people have been involved with the occult or if they have been listening to hard rock type music that this can also open a door for the demonic to enter. Whatever the door may have been; the answer is to receive Jesus and to close those doors completely and then seek for total restoration and healing.

In Luke 5 there was a man who was demon possessed to the point where he had to be chained down because he became so violent. V 5 "night and day among the tombs and in the hills, he would cry out and cut himself with stones".

Here we see an example of self harm which is another part of mental health illnesses. Some people seek to self harm to try to get rid of the pain that is inside of them.

When the man saw Jesus, he came running and fell at his feet crying out "what do you want with me - swear to me that you won't torture me". This was not the man who was speaking but the demons inside him - they knew that their time was up and they had to leave soon. Whenever Jesus shows up, demons have to leave. The demons begged Jesus to be allowed to go into a herd of pigs that was nearby and Jesus gave them permission to do so. After this the man was completely restored and when the people of that town came along, it says that;

V15 "they saw the man who had been possessed by the legion of demons sitting there, dressed and in his right mind and they were afraid".

The man was dressed and he was in his right mind.

2 Timothy 1 v 7 " You did not receive a spirit of fear, but of love, power and a sound mind" (KJV).

God has provided healing not only for our physical bodies and for our emotions but also for our minds - to give us a sound mind.

1 Corinthians 2 v 16 "we have the mind of Christ"

If we have the mind of Christ through the cross, then we have the ability to be stable and to have soundness of mind.

Barriers to Healing

If healing has already been purchased at the cross, then why are some people not healed? This is a very complex question that we may not have all the answers to, but I want us to look at a few of the barriers to healing. As you are reading this if you realise that there are some barriers that you have put up in your life, then decide to repent and pull them down and allow Jesus to come and touch your life afresh today.

Un-belief

We have already seen that many times, Jesus asked people "do you believe that I am able to do this?". So obviously believing and receiving must be linked very closely. (Mathew 21 v 22 "if you believe, you will receive whatever you ask for in prayer"). We have to believe in order to receive. As we mentioned earlier, the bible says that faith comes by hearing (Romans 10 v 17) so the way that we can get more faith is to read what the word says about healing. I pray that by the time you have read this far in the book, that you will now be in no doubt that it is the will of God for you to be healed and that God wants you well. Once we understand and believe that, then faith can begin to rise up inside of us.

Even Jesus was hindered in his ministry when people would not receive him or did not believe that he was able to heal people.

Mathew 13 v 58 "and he did not do many miracles there because of their lack of faith"

Sometimes we think that Jesus can do anything, anywhere, but we see here that when there is un-belief it hinders his work. In my own experience I have been in some meetings, where there seems to be a brick wall and it is hard to breakthrough and see God do anything and then other places it feels like there is an open heaven. God is the same in each place, but it is the openness of the people that is different. God always desires to do miracles, but we have to be open to allowing him to do them. There were times in the Bible when people even asked Jesus to leave their town because they were afraid of the power of God. Sometimes people will say that miracles only happen abroad, but my experience is that I have seen as many miracles in my own country as I have when I have travelled abroad. God does not change because we travel to another nation - the only thing that changes is the hearts of the people. If people are open and willing, then he will move in any nation, anytime, anywhere.

There was a lady in a meeting in this nation a while ago who had been suffering with hearing problems for 30 years. As she sat in the meeting, she could feel faith rising up inside of her even though she was finding it hard to hear what I was speaking about; nevertheless God was moving in her throughout the meeting. When the time of ministry came, she came forward and as she stood in front of me; she declared "I have not been able to hear properly for 30 years, but I know that I am going to be healed right now"! Her faith had risen to such a place, that she knew that this was her day for a miracle. As I placed my hands on her ears, I declared "according to your faith, be it unto you". She was completely healed and could hear normally for the first time in 30 years and not only that, but

God also removed all the pain in her body that she had also been experiencing! She received her miracle not only because of the finished work of the cross but because of her faith.

I compare this to other times, when I have known that God wanted to touch someone but they have refused to get up out of their seat when the call for healing took place and they left the same way that they came in - how sad!

I have also come to know that there are sometimes when God jumps out of our theological boxes. For example; there are times when we have to pray specifically and have words of knowledge and get to the root of a problem and the person has to stand in faith and then there are other times when I may stand on a platform with a big crowd and just release anointing and people get healed - but even then, I believe that there is an atmosphere of faith that is in the place enabling God to work.

Let us then decide that we are going to put aside our un-belief and ask God to increase our faith to believe for a miracle.

Un-forgiveness

When we harbour un-forgiveness and bitterness in our hearts, then it will be a barrier to receiving healing. We looked at earlier how wrong emotions can affect our bodies and cause illnesses to come and take root. In the same way, un-forgiveness will hinder our healing because it puts us in a wrong relationship with God.

In Mathew 18 v 21-35 we read the Parable of the un-merciful servant, where Jesus gives the illustration of a man who has been released from a big debt but then he goes and finds someone who owes him a smaller debt but he refuses to forgive him. We have been forgiven a huge debt on the cross and we are called to forgive others. I know that this is not always easy, especially if it has been a very bad thing that has happened to us and I do not believe that forgiveness is possible in our natural ability; it has to be supernatural ability.

First of all, we need to understand that God would not ask us to do something that he will not help us to do. Secondly we need to understand that forgiveness is not saying that what someone did to us is ok. Sometimes we feel that if we forgive, then that person has got away with something un-punished; almost as if we are holding them in our judgement. Just because we forgive, it doesn't mean that we are saying that what they did was ok, BUT what we are doing is releasing that person out of our hands of judgement and into God's hands. If there is anything to judge, then God will do it. If there has been something serious happen to you, then rest assured that God will judge them either in this life or in the life to come.

Hebrews 10 v 30-31 "It is mine to avenge; I will repay and again the Lord will judge his people. It is a dreadful thing to fall into the hands of the living God".

When we forgive we release the person and the situation into God's hands and we release ourselves, trusting that he will deal with the situation on our behalf. When we live in un-forgiveness then bitterness and anger comes into our lives and causes more pain and devastation to our lives. In v 34 it says "in anger, his master turned him over to the jailers to be tortured, until he should pay back all he owed" v 35 "this is how my heavenly Father will treat each of you unless you forgive your brother from your heart". So when we do not forgive, we are tortured and tormented - this is often how it feels when we live in bitterness. That is also why the root of some arthritis can be bitterness because we are releasing wrong chemicals into our body that affects our joints. When you get angry you can feel your whole body tightening up which you can often feel in your wrists and ankles etc so imagine living constantly like that every day of your life; it will make your body to be permanently twisted.

Forgiving also does not mean that we do not need to seek justice in this world; for example if a crime has been committed against us. I believe that if we have had a crime against us, then it is right for us to seek for justice in the legal courts etc; but it is the attitude in our hearts that we are talking about here. There have been times when we have heard on the TV that someone has forgiven someone because they are a Christian and yet they are still at the trial of a person who may have harmed a family member etc. So let us not confuse forgiveness with not taking any action if necessary. When we forgive we are simply releasing ourselves from the effects of living in bitterness for the rest of our lives.

Although sometimes it may be serious issues that we are holding; there are also many times when we have been holding on to trivial matters and most of the time the other person can't even remember what they have done to upset us. They may be living their lives quite pleasantly, while we are living in torment and anxiety. Many times things started off as a small issue and then it escalates into a huge mountain because we did not deal with it to begin with. Sometimes we can't even remember what the original issue was. In these situations, then we need to forgive and move on and depending on the situation, we may even need to go to the other person and make some reconciliation if it is possible. When we do this, we will find that a great weight has been lifted from off our shoulders.

When we are living in bitterness and anger and un-forgiveness, not only are we tormenting ourselves but we are hindering our healing because we are living in rebellion to how God asked us to live; so we are not placing ourselves in a correct position to receive from him.

Un-forgiveness towards God

Sometimes we can be angry with people but sometimes we can also be angry and have un-forgiveness towards God himself. Maybe something happened and we didn't understand why God allowed it to happen or why he didn't answer a prayer for a loved one; something didn't work out how we hoped that it would. There are many things in this life, that we do not understand, but if we hold anger against God, then how can we then receive healing from him? There are many things that we may be blaming God for that are actually nothing to do with him. Often we suffer because of other peoples free will's and that has nothing to do with God, or the enemy has been allowed to attack our lives for some reason.

I do believe in being real with God (he knows how we feel anyway) so take your feelings to the Lord but in a right way. It is ok to tell God that you are angry with him and that you do not understand what he is doing/has done. BUT let us come with a heart that is wanting God to take those hurts and bring us healing and sometimes we may have to come to a place where we are willing to lay down what we don't understand in order to move forward. Sometimes God explains why things happen and sometimes he doesn't but he will give you peace to accept what you don't understand if you will allow him to.

Forgiving Yourself

Lastly, we can sometimes have un-forgiveness towards ourselves. There are some people who can never forgive themselves for something that they have done in their lives. Maybe something happened that had great consequences; maybe an accident that caused devastating effects for someone and we are saying "why did I do that, why was I not more careful?" Maybe someone we loved has died and we wish that we had spent more time with them or maybe we had an argument and never had time to make it up before they died and now we are living with regrets in our lives and punishing ourselves and not forgiving ourselves. Again these can have awful effects upon our bodies. Maybe we feel that we do not deserve to have anything good happen to us because we feel that we are such an awful person. The truth is that no matter how much we may want to go back and change things - we can't. No amount of tormenting ourselves can change what has already happened. All we can do is to learn from our mistakes and move forward.

If we have truly repented of anything that we have done, then Jesus has forgiven us and we also need to forgive ourselves. This can be a big barrier to healing because when we can't forgive ourselves, then we believe the lie, that our sickness is our punishment, it is what we deserve. The truth is that God has forgiven you and he wants to heal and to restore you. It is true that some things may have life time consequences but it is also true that God can turn all situations around for good if we will allow him to. Allow God to take the regrets from your life and bring his emotional healing into your life.

Sin

Another barrier to healing is sin in our lives. As we saw at the beginning of this book, the source of all original sickness was because of sin in the garden of Eden. In the same way, our own sin can cause sickness and also be a barrier to healing. We need to check to make sure that we are not deliberately living in rebellion to God and his ways if we want to be healed. It is interesting that sometimes when Jesus prayed for people to be healed, he said "your sins are forgiven" almost as if, sin was the root of the sickness. In Luke 5 v 20 when the friends brought the paralysed man to Jesus he said to him "friend, your sins are forgiven" and then later in v 24 he said "take up your mat and go home". He got to the most important need first and then physical healing followed. I do not believe that God uses sickness to punish us if we are sin as we looked at earlier, but when we are in sin, we are vulnerable to the attacks of the enemy.

How to receive your healing

We have seen that healing is already a finished work; so how do we receive that healing into our body? There can be many different ways that we can receive healing. We can receive healing in our own home directly from God through prayer; or we can receive healing by standing on the word and quoting the healing scriptures into our bodies every day. We can take authority ourselves over sickness in our bodies and we can speak to our bodies and tell them to come in line with the word of God. We can also receive by attending a healing service and having a minister of God lay hands on us. We can receive by doing practical things to improve our life style or by forgiving or dealing with wrong emotions.

Standing on the word

One of the most powerful ways that we can receive healing is by standing on the word of God ourselves for our healing. When you read through the bible and get all the healing scriptures and then begin to meditate upon them and speak them into your body, I believe that symptoms in your body will begin to change and come in line with the word of God.
Isaiah 55 v 11 "so is my word that goes out from my mouth, it will not return to me empty but will accomplish what I desire"

When we speak God's word into our lives, into our bodies, into our situations, then our circumstances have to change to match what the word is saying. God's word will not return empty but will accomplish what it says it will do. Even when Jesus was in the wilderness and the devil came to try to tempt him at his weakest moment, he overcame by saying "it is written" and the devil left him. Our feelings can change day by day and we can be tempted to speak negative things into our lives, but the word is un-changeable through all storms of life and it has power to change situations.

Romans 4 v 17 "the God who gives life to the dead and calls things that are not as though they were".

Here it says that God actually speaks about things as if they are even when they are not yet manifested in the natural realm! If we are sick, then as we stand on the word and speak the word, we can also speak to our bodies and tell them that they are healed and healthy. This is not denying facts; it is simply speaking truth into facts and calling them to change into truth. We are calling the things that are not as if they were and one day we will find that they actually become real in the natural realm. The truth is that we are already healed in the spiritual realm because Jesus did it all on the cross, but we are calling that truth from the heavenly realms into the earthly realm.

There are many ways that we can receive and the key is to ask the Lord how he wants to work in our life and situation. Then when we have received, we need to hold on to our healing.

Holding on to your healing

It is one thing to be healed; it is another to stay healed and to walk in health. I have sometimes seen people get healed in a meeting but then a few weeks/months later they may get sick again and I think "Why? - you were healed". I have come to realise that we need to teach people not only how to get healed but also how to walk in their healing and to stay healed. When God heals us, sometimes the enemy wants to come to steal away the blessing that we have received and to deceive us that we were not really healed. Let me tell you that if Jesus has healed you, then you are really healed. This is why it is important that we understand the teachings concerning what the word says about healing so we can stand and hold on to our healing and not let it be stolen from us. The very first words that the devil spoke in Genesis 3 v 1 was; "Did God really say?". Today he still uses those same words, "Did God really heal you?". If we have been healed and then we are going back into a church that does not believe in healing or we have friends who are sceptical, then we can begin to listen to their lies and start to doubt our own healing. We need to be able to stand on the word and say "Yes, I am healed by the stripes of Jesus and no weapon formed against me shall prosper". If the enemy tries to bring symptoms of what you were healed from back, then stand in faith and declare that you are healed by using the scriptures concerning healing and rebuke the sickness in Jesus name.

We also need to make sure that we are following the Lord and not walking in sin in our lives or else the enemy has a legal foothold to come and take our healing away.

Mathew 12 v 43-45 "When an evil spirit comes out of a man it goes through arid places seeking rest and does not find it. Then it says, I will return to the house I left. When it arrives, it finds the house un-occupied, swept clean and put in order. Then it takes with it seven other spirits more wicked than itself and they go in and live there. And the final condition of that man is worse than the first".

Here Jesus was speaking about when an evil spirit comes out of someone, it is seeking for somewhere else to go and eventually it decides to try to return from where it was first cast out from. When it returns it finds the house un-occupied - there was a vacuum - no one else was living there - there was space. So it calls seven other spirits more wicked than itself and tells them "I have found a place where we can all live" and the final condition of that person is worse than before.

I believe that this speaks of a person who has been set free and healed but because their lives have been left empty - they have not filled their hearts and lives with the presence of God; then they have an open door for the enemy to return and even to make them worse!

If we have had a situation where we have had deliverance especially, then we need to make sure that afterwards we receive prayer to be filled with the Holy Spirit and that we then live our lives in such a way that the enemy has no right to try to return.

When Jesus healed the man by the pool of Bethesda, he then found him later on and he said to him

John 5 v 14 "See you are well again, stop sinning or something worse may happen to you".

We are not told what the man was doing or what his sin was; but Jesus obviously knew that he was in sin and he was warning him that if he didn't stop, that not only might he lose his healing; but that something even worse may happen. Just like the un-occupied house, he might end up 7 times worse than before he started.

So after we have been healed, we have a responsibility to walk in our healing by standing in faith and also by living correctly.

John 8 v 1-11 Jesus meets a lady who is caught in adultery and all the elders want to stone her. However Jesus has compassion on her and says to the people in v 7 "if anyone of you is without sin, let him be the first to cast a stone at her". Slowly all the people left leaving only Jesus standing there - he was the only one who had the right to condemn her and yet he didn't condemn her, he released her BUT then he says to her;

v11 "Then neither do I condemn you Jesus declared. Go now, and leave your life of sin".
He released her and gave her another chance, but then he instructs her to leave her life of sin. God's grace and mercy demands a change in our lives.

If we have been healed of a sickness that was caused because of a wrong lifestyle; then when we are healed, we need to also change our lifestyle or else that sickness can come back. For example if we had cancer because we smoked and God graciously healed us; he does not expect us to carry on smoking!

I want to encourage you today as you have read about the healing power of God, that if you need healing in your life, then reach out right now and receive that healing from the Lord. I want you to see the sickness that is in your body nailed to the cross and then see the healing from Jesus flowing back to you from the cross.

Determine today to not only seek to be healed, but to walk in health.

SECTION 2 - HOW TO PRAY FOR THE SICK

CHAPTER 6

HOW DID JESUS AND THE APOSTLES HEAL THE SICK?

Mark 16 v 18 "They will place their hands on sick people and they will get well"

The great commission is not only to preach the gospel but also to heal the sick. When Jesus sent out his disciples, he sent them to preach the gospel and to heal the sick (Luke 9 v 2)

I want us to look in this section about how we can also be used by God to heal the sick. First of all I want us to see that Jesus did not call us to "pray" for the sick, he called us to "heal" them; and there is a big difference. One is asking God to do something and the other is us taking and using the authority that we have been given in his name and enforcing the finished work of the cross. Many times I hear people praying "Oh Lord, if it be thy will, heal this person"! I can not even come into agreement to say "amen" to that prayer, because as we looked at earlier, we know that it is always God's will to heal someone and he has given us all power and all authority to speak that healing in his name.

In Luke 10 v 9 when he sent out the 72 disciples he told them "heal the sick who are there". Jesus expected that if they found sick people in the towns where they were preaching, that they would heal them.

Luke 9 v 6 "so they set out and went from village to village preaching the gospel and healing people everywhere".

When the original 12 went out; they went out with power and authority and they healed people everywhere. Today we are called with the same power and authority; in fact even more so; because we are now living after the victory of the cross. Jesus said;

John 14 v 12 "anyone who has faith in me will do what I have been doing. He will do even greater things than these because I am going to the Father".

Jesus said that not only can we do the same as he did, but even greater - why? Because he has now won the victory, gone back to the Father and now the Holy Spirit has been poured out on every believer for the purpose of preaching the gospel and healing the sick. Preaching the gospel and healing and deliverance go together, you can not separate them. Jesus said

Mark 16 v 17 "these signs shall accompany those who believe"

When we preach the gospel there will be signs following our words. Every meeting where I speak about healing, I expect to see Jesus heal people. There was a lady in a meeting recently who had had a hernia operation and was left with ripped scar tissue that wouldn't heal and was causing her a lot of pain; as she came forward, she said that she felt fire go through her body and she was completely healed and free from pain.

Another time when we were in India recently, we saw amazing

miracles following the preaching of the gospel and as the people saw the miracles, they knew that Jesus was real and they began to come forward to give their lives to the Lord. One man came and asked me to pray for him to be healed. I asked him if he knew Jesus and he said "No". Then I asked him if he wanted to know Jesus and he replied that he would like me to pray for him to be healed. I knew that he was wanting to know "is your God real?". So I prayed for him and God healed him! Then he also got saved! God will always confirm the gospel with signs for his glory. Another time, I felt to stop half way through my message and to ask how many people were suffering with back pain. Quite a few people put their hands up. I then instructed them to stand up so that I could pray for them. As I prayed for them to be healed, many of them came forward to say that pain had left their bodies. I then continued on with the message and began to call people for salvation. I believe that the Lord led me to do this, so that the people would know that Jesus is real. In some of these countries they have many gods and yet the people are hungry to know who God really is and when they see a demonstration of the power of God, then they are ready to receive and follow him.

Some of the testimonies that we have been receiving back from the pastor's recently include the following; abdomen and pain in womb healed, heart and lung problems healed, knee pains healed, arthritis healed, thyroid problems healed, spinal problems healed, hips healed, diabetes healed, blood pressure healed, eye sight restored, chest pains healed, set free from alcohol addiction, asthma healed and many many more ... these are just a few of the testimonies that have been coming through from our recent mission - God is still doing miracles today and confirming his word.

Another time in Uganda, the Lord gave me a word of knowledge that there was someone with a breast tumour and he was going to heal them. Suddenly I saw a lady who was under the power of the Holy Spirit in the meeting and I knew that it was her. I began to pray and called her to come to the front; when she came to the front she began to tell me that she had been due to go to the hospital soon for an operation, but now the tumour had completely shrunk! Praise God.

For any who may be reading this book and thinking that miracles only happen abroad, I want to tell you that I have seen as many miracles in England as I have seen abroad. God does not change because we go abroad - he is the same God here as anywhere. I remember several years ago, I went back to a meeting to preach in this country and a lady was there who had been there the previous year and she began to tell me her testimony. The previous year when I was there, I had prayed for her. She was due to go to hospital the next day to have a tumour removed but as she received prayer that night, she knew that she was healed. Nevertheless she went along to the hospital the next day as planned but as they did a pre-scan to check where the tumour was, they discovered that there was no tumour! Praise God.

I remember once someone asked me to pray for them to receive the anointing and then they told me that they had seen miracles when they went to Africa but now they don't see them here. I told them that God was the same here and that they should expect to see the same things here. I have actually been very encouraged because I began to see miracles first in my own country before I even went to Africa and I am so pleased that I did because it proves that God is the same anywhere as long as we believe.

I want us to look in this section to see how Jesus prayed for the sick and to parallel this with how the apostles prayed for the sick and to encourage you that we also are to pray and see people healed in Jesus name.

How did Jesus pray for the sick

As we look throughout the gospels we see that there were many ways that Jesus healed the sick and then as we parallel these with how the apostles healed the sick, we see that there are many similarities between them. The apostles had learnt from the master and he had passed his authority on to them. Today we also, are called to go and heal the sick with the authority that we have been given in Jesus name. This authority is not just for a few select people but it is available for every believer who will walk with the Lord in holiness and a desire to serve him. Now we will begin to look at a few scriptures where Jesus healed the sick and see the different ways that he prayed. I believe that in every situation we need to be open to how the Holy Spirit is directing us to pray because God will not stick to a formula; just when we think we have got it all worked out; he will change his plan and ask us to do something different. The method is not important; it is the result that we are looking for. Sometimes Jesus healed by laying hands on people, sometimes he healed people by speaking the word and sometimes he healed just by his presence being there. In all of the instances, it is his authority that is the main factor - the sicknesses had to leave because they knew that he had authority over them.

Command and Touch

Luke 4 v 38-39 "Simon's mother in law was suffering from a high fever so they asked Jesus to help her. So he bent over her and rebuked the fever and it left her".

Mathew 8 v 15 "he touched her hand and the fever left her"

Here Jesus uses the command of rebuke and the power of touch to the sickness and <u>immediately</u> it had to obey and leave. Then in v 40 it says

"when the sun was setting, the people brought to Jesus all who had various kinds of sickness, and laying his hands on each one, he healed them".

Now word had got around that Jesus was healing people, so the crowds brought all their sick friends and relatives to Jesus and it says that he laid his hands on each one of them and they were <u>immediately</u> healed. There is power in the touch of Jesus. When we speak the word and touch people with the anointing of God, then something powerful will happen and people will be healed. Jesus used both word and touch to bring healing.

Acts 9 v 17 -18 Is the story where the disciple Ananias is asked by the Lord to go and pray for Saul who had become blind after being knocked off his horse on the road to Damascus. Ananias goes to him and tells him that God has sent him to restore his sight. Then he places his hands on him and the bible says that; something like scales fell from his eyes and he could see again. Here the disciple used the power of both speaking what God was going to do and then touching Saul's eyes to bring about the healing and restoration that was required. Whenever I pray for people, I will always speak something as well as whatever else the Lord is leading me to do; whether that is to lay hands or if in a bigger meeting, I may simply speak from the platform and release the anointing. Often I will ask the people to place their own hands on the affected area and then I will pray and release the healing power of God over them. In each incident there is an element of speech and touch.

Mark 7 v 32-35 Here the people bring to Jesus a man who was deaf and could hardly speak. Jesus took the man aside and put his fingers into his ears and then he spat and touched the man's tongue. Then he looked up to heaven and said "Ephphatha" which means "be opened" and the man's ears were opened and his tongue was loosed and he could speak normally. Here again we see the combination of both speaking and touching and commanding. I have prayed for several people who have had hearing problems and as I have placed my fingers into their ears and commanded their ears to open, then they have received their hearing. We are continuing on following the pattern of how Jesus prayed for the sick.

His Presence

There were many times when just the presence of Jesus was enough to heal the sick without him seemingly doing anything. I believe that we can get to the place if we walk close enough with God, that our presence can also heal the sick. I have always believed that if we could just bring the presence of God into a meeting, then people would get healed without anyone laying hands on anyone. Then a few years ago, I was in a meeting where the glory of God began to fall and I didn't even get to preach. In that glory of God people began to get healed. There was one lady who had come into the meeting who had Oestoarthritis and was on crutches. She had been told that there was nothing that could be done for her except taking pain killers. As the presence of God filled that room, she suddenly announced that she had been healed! No-body was near her except God. She threw her crutches away and came to the front of the meeting to testify that God had healed her. After that several other people also began to come forward to testify that pain had left their bodies as we were standing in the presence of God.

Luke 6 v 19 "the people all tried to touch him because power was coming from him and healing them all"

Here Jesus had come to speak to the people and there was so much power coming out of him that people were getting healed just sitting listening to his words. I believe that this was for two reasons; one - obviously Jesus was carrying power from on high but also the word of God carries power and as they listened to the word, power was there to confirm his word. I have had many situations where I have had people testify that as they have been sitting listening to the word that they experienced healing in their bodies taking place.

Psalm 107 v 20 "he sent forth his word and healed them"

The word of God has healing and Jesus is the word made flesh among us - so the very word of God was speaking in their midst and they were all getting healed. The word has power to heal. That is why as we speak the truth of the word over our lives and over those that we pray for, we will see amazing things happening. I have had people tell me that they came into a meeting not able to hear properly but as they sat under the word of God, suddenly their hearing was restored - others have testified that pain left their bodies. One lady came at the end of a meeting to tell me that she had been left with a lump on her shoulder after an injury that had not healed properly. But as she sat under the presence of the Lord, she suddenly realised that the lump had gone and her shoulder was now completely smooth again!

Acts 5 v 12 "the apostles performed many miraculous signs and wonders among the people".

Acts 5 v 15 "as a result, people brought the sick into the streets and laid them on beds and mats so that at least Peter's shadow might fall on some of them as he passed by. Crowds gathered also from the towns around Jerusalem bringing their sick and those tormented by evil spirits and all of them were healed".

Wow! Here the people began to notice that the apostles were doing many miracles and so they begin to bring all the sick to them so that even Peter's shadow might fall on them as he passed by. They saw that these apostles were carrying something called "glory" on their lives, they were carrying the presence of God and they believed that even if the sick could get near to them, then they would be healed. I was in a meeting once where a lady told me afterwards that even as she walked into the meeting she could feel fire coming from me from the other side of the room and later on in the meeting she got healed. If Peter's shadow could heal the sick, then what about our shadow? I believe that the reason why Peter's shadow could heal the sick was because he was walking so close to the Lord that the shadow, was actually the shadow of the Holy Spirit!

Touching Jesus

Mathew 14 v 35-36 "and when the men of that place recognised Jesus, they sent word to all the surrounding country. People brought all their sick to him and begged him to let the sick just touch the edge of his cloak and <u>all</u> who touched him were healed".

Here the people recognised the power of Jesus and they knew that if they could just touch him then they would be healed. There are some countries were I have been to that people will literally be running after us just trying to touch us believing that they will be healed. In these situations, we always direct the people's attention to Jesus for it is him who is the healer and we are simply the vessels but the people are seeing anointing and they want to touch the power of God for their miracle.

When people recognise that Jesus is doing something, then they will run to that place. Again in India recently, we were having our lunch at the pastor's house after the morning session of a conference and suddenly people began arriving at the house where we were eating and they were queuing up to receive prayer. Between first and second course of lunch, we saw people saved, baptised in the Holy Spirit and healed including a lady who saw a tumour under her arm disappear!! They had heard that Jesus was in town and they wanted to receive a miracle.

I believe that in a meeting there can be many people who are worshipping God but then there may be a few who are really touching the heart of God.

Luke 8 v 43-44 "and a woman was there who had been subject to bleeding for twelve years but no-one could heal her. She came up behind him and touched the edge of his cloak and immediately her bleeding stopped".

12 years of pain and suffering ended because she touched Jesus. We often talk about the Lord touching us; but there is also a place where we touch Jesus. This lady was an out-cast, un-clean because of her bleeding. She should not have even been in a public place and yet she had decided that she would not let her miracle pass by and she pushed through the crowd to touch Jesus.

Speaking the word

We saw earlier about the power of the spoken word and many times, Jesus spoke a word and the people were healed. I believe that there is no distance in the spirit and even if we are praying for someone that is on the other side of the world, we can simply proclaim the word over that person's life, we can take authority over the sickness and command it to go in Jesus name and that sickness has to obey us just like it obeyed Jesus.

Mathew 8 v 5-13 is the story of the centurion who came to Jesus asking him to heal his servant who was seriously ill at home.

V 8 "Just say the word and my servant will be healed"

V 13 "Go, it will be done just as you believed it would. And his servant was healed at that very hour".

Here the centurion understands about the power of authority and he realises that Jesus does not even need to come to his house, he only needs to speak the word and the sickness will obey and leave. Jesus was amazed at such great faith and told the man that it would be done for him just as he believed and the servant was healed at that very moment.

In Luke 5 v 20-25 he speaks to the paralysed man and he says to him "pick up your mat and go home". He speaks his word to the man and the man is completely healed.

Acts 9 v 33-35 "There he found a man named Aeneas, a paralytic who had been bedridden for eight years. "Aeneas, Peter said to him, "Jesus Christ heals you. Get up and tidy up your mat. Immediately Aeneas got up. All those who lived in Lydda and Sharon saw him and turned to the Lord".

Here Paul was travelling around the country and he came across this man called Aeneas who had been paralysed for 8 years. He doesn't lay hands on him, he simply declares the truth of the spoken word to him and tells him that Jesus Christ heals him and to pick up his mat. Immediately the man is healed and 2 whole towns have revival!

I believe that the key to revival is miracles - when people see the miraculous then they will turn to the Lord. We have seen this as we have travelled in other countries; that when miracles begin to take place, people give their lives to the Lord.

Handkerchiefs

Another way of praying for people who may not be present is to anoint handkerchiefs or any article that can be taken to the person and placed upon them for healing.

Acts 19 v 11-12 "God did extraordinary miracles through Paul so that even handkerchiefs and aprons that had touched him were taken to the sick and their illnesses were cured and evil spirits left them"

Here it actually doesn't even say that Paul prayed on the

articles, it just says that they had touched him. So much was the power of God coming from him, that anything that had been near him carried power! Many times in a meeting people will bring tissues, handkerchiefs, even articles of clothing for me to pray over and I have seen God doing miracles through this.

One testimony that I heard recently was from a lady who had brought me a tissue to pray over 12 years ago because her daughter was having a baby and the scan was showing that it had a deformity. I prayed over the tissue and gave it back to the mother. She went and gave the prayer tissue to her daughter and prayed concerning the baby. I found out 12 years later that the baby had been born completely healthy with no deformity at all and was now a healthy 12 year old child - Praise God!

Anointing with oil

Another way that we can pray for the sick is by anointing them with oil in the name of the Lord.

Mark 6 v 13 "They drove out many demons and anointed many sick people with oil and healed them".

Oil is symbolic of the anointing and sometimes the Lord may direct you to use oil as you pray for people.

James 5 v 14-15" Is anyone of you sick? He should call the elders of the church to pray over him and anoint him with oil in the name of the Lord. And the prayer offered in faith will make the sick person well."

Notice here that it says that the prayer offered <u>in faith</u> will make the sick person well. The right formulas of using oil, laying hands, speaking the word will not work effectively unless we are offering our prayer in faith and believing that God is going to do something. This is why we need to get a good understanding of the word of God concerning healing so that we can pray in faith, taking the authority that has been given to us.

<u>Raising the Dead</u>

Luke 7 v 11-16 is the story where Jesus goes to a funeral and turns a day of mourning into a day of rejoicing. He goes to a town called Nain where a funeral is taking place of a widow who has now lost her only son.

V13 "when the Lord saw her, his heart went out to her and he said "don't cry" . Then he went up and touched the coffin and those carrying it stood still. He said "young man, I say to you, get up" The dead man sat up and began to talk and Jesus gave him back to his mother".

What an amazing day that must have been - it started off as a disaster but it ended with a miracle.

Acts 9 v 40 "Peter sent them all out of the room; then he got down on his knees and prayed. Turning towards the dead woman, he said "Tabitha get up". She opened her eyes and seeing Peter she sat up".
Here Peter does a very similar miracle and he simply prays and then tells the dead woman to wake up just like Jesus spoke to

the boy in the coffin. Remember that Peter had walked with Jesus and seen the miracles that he had done and now he was continuing the work of his Lord in the same way. Even in the Old Testament Elijah and Elisha were used to raise the dead - (1 Kings 17 v 19-23 & 2 Kings 4 v 32-35).

We also have been called to carry on the works of the Lord which can include raising the dead if the Lord directs us to do so. I do believe though that un-like healing, raising the dead is when we are specifically called by the Lord to do it rather than just thinking we can go and empty the morgue! In those times, there comes a supernatural anointing of boldness and authority for that time.

Deliverance

When we are praying for people, we may often find that there is more than physical healing that is needed and it may be deliverance from an evil spirit that needs to take place. Some sicknesses as we looked at earlier may be caused by spirits of infirmity or spirits of blindness, deafness etc and we need the discernment of the Holy Spirit to know how to pray for the breakthrough.

In Mathew 17 v 15-18 a man brings his son to Jesus because he is having seizures and falling into the fire.

V18 "Jesus rebuked the demon and it came out of the boy and he was healed from that moment". Here the root of the problem was a demonic spirit which needed to be cast out.

Mathew 8 v 16 "he drove out the spirits with a word"

Here we see that Jesus did not need to take a long time with deliverance, he simply spoke a word and the spirits had to obey. Sometimes we find that a lot of deliverance is more the enemy putting on a show. If we are walking in power and authority then deliverance should not be difficult.

Luke 10 v 1 "he gave them authority to drive out evil spirits and to heal every disease and sickness"

Here Jesus puts deliverance and healing together and the same authority and anointing covers both of them. If we have anointing to heal, then we have anointing to cast out spirits. We do need though to make sure that we are living our lives right before the Lord or else we will not be able to do deliverance and in fact; it can be dangerous to attempt it if we are living in sin and not in a right relationship with God.

In Acts 19 v 13-16 we read a story about seven sons of Sceva who were trying to cast out demons by speaking the name of Jesus whom Paul preaches. They were using a formula that they had heard Paul using, but they did not have a relationship with Jesus and the demons knew that they had no authority to be casting them out. Let me advise you that if you have no real relationship with God or you don't fully understand what you are doing, then leave deliverance alone because we can cause more harm to ourselves and to the person that we are praying for instead of helping them.

V 15 "one day the evil spirit answered them "Jesus I know and I know about Paul, but who are you?. Then the man who had the evil spirit jumped on them and overpowered them all. He gave them such a beating that they ran out of the house naked and bleeding".

Here one demon possessed man overpowered 7 other men who didn't know what they were doing. There is a lesson in there for us. If you belong to Christ and are walking in his power and authority, then demons must obey our words and can not overpower us; BUT if we have no relationship with God and no authority and are just using religious words that we have heard in a book or seen from someone else then we are on dangerous ground.

How can we know if deliverance is needed when praying for someone?

The most obvious answer to this is that the Holy Spirit will witness to you when you begin to pray. At other times, you may begin to pray and then the person will begin to manifest and you know that you are now dealing with a demonic spirit. Sometimes if people tell me that the pain in their body keeps moving from place to place, then I often discern that a spirit is involved. In all these instances, we just need to be led by the Holy Spirit and pray how the Lord leads us, taking authority and rebuking anything demonic and commanding it to leave in Jesus name. If you are still un-sure what to pray, you can pray in tongues knowing that you are praying the will of God.

Sometimes just bringing people into the presence of God is enough for them to be delivered. I did a meeting in Uganda recently where I saw people coming into the presence of God and God was delivering them and setting them free just by his presence without any human intervention. It was something glorious to watch!

Creative Miracles

We looked at the story earlier where Jesus spat on the ground, made mud and put it on the man's eyes and told him to go and wash in Siloam and he came home seeing (John 9 v 6-7). As I explained earlier, I believe that this was a creative miracle of new eyes being made from the mud and placed into the man's eye sockets. I believe that we need to expect God to use us to do creative miracles. Many times when I have been praying for people I have seen the angels going back into heaven to get a new body part for someone. I believe that there are storehouses in heaven with every available body part that we might ever need and the angels can go and get them when people pray in faith and believe for them. The God who created us in our mother's womb (Psalm 139) and made every part of our body, is the same God who is able to re-create new body parts if we have need of them throughout our lives. There is nothing that is impossible for God. We have the greatest surgeon of all!

CHAPTER 7

THE HOLY SPIRT AND HEALING

Acts 1 v 8 "But you will receive power when the Holy Spirit comes on you".

For all ministry, we need the presence and power of the Holy Spirit upon our lives. Even Jesus made himself dependant upon the Holy Spirit during his time on earth. We do not see Jesus doing any miracles until after the Holy Spirit had come upon him at his baptism. But after that, we see him healing people everywhere. If we want to see the sick healed, then I believe that we not only have to believe and confess the word but we must have an intimate relationship with the Holy Spirit.

Luke 5 v 17 "and the power of the Lord was present for him to heal the sick".

Who was present to heal the sick? Who is this passage referring to?
Jesus was there in person, the Father is always in heaven, so this must have been referring to the Holy Spirit who was present for Jesus to be able to heal the sick. Does that mean that if the Holy Spirit was not present, then Jesus could not have done any miracles? Surely he was the Son of God? And yet, he had made a partnership with the Holy Spirit and they were working together. We too, need to make a partnership to work together with the Holy Spirit. When the Holy Spirit turns up, then miracles begin to happen. There have been many times, when I have

stood in the presence of the Lord and watched him doing miracles and it is an amazing experience. Before every meeting, I always ask the Holy Spirit to come and take control of everything that is going to take place, giving him free reign in the place to do whatever he wants to do.

I believe that the key to the Holy Spirit showing up in a meeting is not just asking him to come, but it is the depth of our relationship with him in our personal lives on a daily basis. Imagine for a minute about relationships in the natural sense. If you have a really close relationship with a friend/family member etc and then you phone them up at short notice asking them to come to see you; they are more likely to drop other plans and try to accommodate you if they have a good relationship with you. If you are just a distant friend, then they may tell you that they already have other plans for that time and can you re-schedule for another more convenient time. If we are close to the Holy Spirit then he is with us everywhere we go, flowing out from us and when we call upon his name - he hears his friend calling him and his presence is immediate in that place.

The Gifts of the Spirit

In 1 Corinthians 12 v 4-11 it lists all the gifts of the Holy Spirit and I believe that we need the gifts of the Spirit to be able to operate in healing.

V 11 "he gives them to each one just as he determines"

Here it is telling us that the Holy Spirit has all of these 9 gifts and that he is the one who chooses whom to give them to.

V 8 "to one there is given through the spirit, the message of wisdom, to another the message of knowledge by means of the same spirit, to another faith by the same spirit, to another gifts of healing by that one spirit, to another miraculous powers, to another prophecy, to another distinguishing between spirits, to another speaking in different kinds of tongues, and to still another the interpretation of tongues"

I believe that it is possible to have all of the gifts in our lives and then we just bring out each one as it is needed in each different ministry situation. For example, we may be praying for someone and they tell us that they have a heart condition. So now, we need the gift of healing, but we also need the gift of faith to believe that the prayer will work but we may also need a gift of knowledge because the heart condition has a under-lying problem connected to it that has caused the heart condition. Many times when Jesus prayed for people he got right to the root of their situation and instead of praying for healing, he would say things like "your sins are forgiven" or "go and call your husband" when he knew that the woman had no husband. He went straight to the root of their real need and in doing so, they were then completely healed and restored and made whole. Jesus wants us to be whole, physically, emotionally and spiritually in every way. So many times we may need to operate in several gifts at once when praying for someone. We may also need the gift of distinguishing between spirits to know whether this it is a demonic spirit that we are dealing with when praying for someone to be healed.

Notice also that it speaks about gift__s__ of healing - meaning that there is more than one gift of healing. As we looked at earlier, there are many different types of healing. Some people are gifted to pray for physical healing and then there may be other people who are more gifted to pray for emotional healing and have a gift in sitting with people in a counselling type of way. This can be a totally different kind of healing, to the healing that would be done in big meeting but it is another gift from God. There are some people who are more comfortable sitting on a one to one basis with someone talking and listening to them and many people need this kind of healing in their lives. Then there are others who feel more comfortable standing on a platform. We are all called with unique abilities and talents and as we embrace our different gifts, then the body of Christ will begin to work in unity together. We all need one another's gifts and we should value and encourage one another in our different abilities. There are some people who are more gifted in the area of deliverance and will specialise in this ministry. There are many ministries where people will go to because they are needing more in-depth counselling or deliverance in their lives and again these are all important and needed.

1 Corinthians 12 v 12 "the body is a unit, though it is made up of many parts; and though all it's parts are many, they form one body".

Notice that it also lists miraculous powers as a separate gift to healing. Often we think that they are the same, but here it lists them as two separate things, so what is the different between a healing and a miracle?

I believe that a healing is something where God intervenes to make a recovery come quicker but it could have been done by a medical route. However, a miracle is something that only God could have done. For example, when blind eyes open, that is a miracle. There is no cure for total blindness - without the supernatural intervention of God, that person will remain blind for the rest of their lives. A leg or an arm growing is a supernatural miracle. Although the advances of medicine today can give people artificial limbs, they can not make a new arm or leg grow but God can - this is a miracle. Raising the dead is a miracle - only possible by the supernatural intervention of God. Even casting out demons could be listed under miracles because it is not possible by any other way than the power of God. Apart from healing there are other things that could be listed under this such as; power over the weather; like when Elijah prayed and it didn't rain for three and a half years and how God led him to the brook to be fed by the ravens, the example of the widow's oil that didn't run out - these were all miracles that wouldn't normally happen. I believe that in these end times, we are going to see more and more miracles taking place for the glory of God.

How to Pray

Many people want to know "how can I pray and see the sick healed?". I believe that the first answer to this is to "BEGIN TO PRAY".

We will never see anything until we step out in faith and begin. Sometimes we are put off because we don't think that we know enough or we don't think that we have enough faith or we worry about what happens if we pray and the person is not healed - will we look silly or be discouraged? I have come to the conclusion that although we may not have all the answers as to why some people are not healed - I do know this. More people will be healed if we pray, than if we do not! Simple !

So, we need to believe that the price for healing has been paid for on the cross and the work is already completed. Then we need to believe that all power and all authority has been given to every believer to lay hands on the sick. Then we need to take a hold of those truths and step out in faith and find someone to pray for - which shouldn't be too hard as there are many sick people everywhere.

First of all we need to speak to the person to find out what they are wanting God to do and what they are believing God for - Jesus always asked people what they wanted. We can not assume what someone may want - just because they can't walk very well, that may not be what they actually want prayer for. If they are un-sure about God's willingness to heal, then we can encourage them with the truth of what the word says about healing, helping them to have faith to believe for healing. Always invite the Holy Spirit into the situation, asking for his help on how to pray and to show you if there is any under-lying issues that you need to get to the root of. Then begin to pray always in the name of Jesus taking authority over the sickness and commanding it to go. After you have prayed, ask the person how they are feeling. Do not be discouraged if they say that they do not feel any different or feel only slightly improved.

Never be afraid to pray again (even Jesus had to pray more than once for a blind man). If they still do not feel any different then encourage them to keep standing in faith and to keep reading healing scriptures. Just because someone doesn't feel any different, it does not mean that they are not healed - when we pray - something must happen. As I shared earlier, I have had situations where I have prayed and at the time it seemed that nothing happened and the person went away in pain, but then a few hours later, suddenly all the pain left. I don't know why this happens, but sometimes it does and we need to encourage people to not become discouraged if an instant miracle is not evident. I always pray believing for an instant miracle and I believe that is how we should pray and what we should believe for; but if for whatever reason, it doesn't happen, then don't be discouraged.

If the person says that they feel different, then encourage them to do something that they couldn't do before; ie; lift up their arm, leg, walk etc and as they do that, the fullness of the healing will manifest itself in their bodies. Before they leave, encourage them that they need to walk in their healing and not allow it to be stolen from them - encourage them to keep reading healing scriptures etc. Never advise someone to stop taking prescribed medicines as this can be dangerous. If they know that they are healed, then advise them to go back to their doctor for a check and for confirmation that they no longer need their medication.

Do not be put off if you do not see great miracles on your first attempt - sometimes we have to keep going in order to see the breakthrough. I want to encourage you that although I believed all of these things for a long time, I spent many years not seeing many people healed as far as I know but then suddenly I got a breakthrough and now I see people healed in nearly every meeting that I do. Someone asked me once "what did you do differently?" and my answer was "nothing". God just broke out one day and it has been flowing ever since. I believe that all those years I was sowing and sowing and sowing and eventually there was a breakthrough that took place.

The more that you pray for people, the bolder you will become. Always follow the leading of the Holy Spirit and ask for his anointing. There have been times, when I have been in a meeting and suddenly I will look at someone and faith rises up inside of me and I know that that person is going to be healed. I believe that the faith can be on the person who is praying, on the person who is receiving or at times both. As long as faith is flowing somewhere, then something will happen.

So I want to encourage you today to step out in faith and to begin to see the sick healed in Jesus name.

Prayer

Father in the name of Jesus, I thank you for every person who has read this book and I ask you right now to release healing anointing into their lives. I speak healing into their bodies, minds and emotions and I speak the finished work of the cross into their lives - that by the stripes of Jesus they are healed. I pray that you will give them fresh revelation concerning healing and that faith will rise up inside of them to receive their healing. I pray also that they may know that they have power and authority to be able to go and heal the sick themselves and I release a fresh anointing of boldness and power upon their lives to be able to go and see miracles in Jesus name. Amen

If you have been encouraged by this book, please write and let us know. You can also visit our website to find details of conferences and healing meetings that you can attend. womenariseministries.net

www.ingramcontent.com/pod-product-compliance
Lightning Source LLC
Chambersburg PA
CBHW072057290426
44110CB00014B/1715